The Way

HOME

The Way
HOME

A Celebration of

Sea Islands Food

and Family with

over 100 Recipes

KARDEA BROWN

AMISTAD

An Imprint of HarperCollinsPublishers

This book is dedicated to my beautiful mother and grandmother.

CONTENTS

Introduction   *1*

New Gullah   28

Sweet Treats   80

Sides, Salads, and More   226

Beverages   266

The sounds. The rhythms. The smells.
When I was coming up, the kitchen gave me life. But, cousins, I wasn't really al-lowed to cook as a kid. My mom and grandma, and in fact everyone I knew on the Sea Islands of South Carolina, expected children to do children's things. The kitchen was no place for kids.

Rooted in Gullah Geechee tradition, we were old-school to the core. Deeply connected to the land and water around Wadmalaw Island, my girlhood—and my womanhood—was steeped in all the cultural rituals of West Africa that our enslaved descendants were able to preserve. And surprisingly, there was much intact. Also, spirituality ran deep—mostly Christian beliefs but with elements of some African practices—and incorporated values like community over indi-viduality, respect for elders, kinship bonds, and honoring the extension of life as well as the afterlife.

And cousins, if you know me, you know Gullah Geechee food traditions. They are the foundation of southern cooking, as far as I'm concerned. Even as a little girl, whether I was coming home from school and having a snack or watching my mom and grandmother make Thanksgiving dinner, I was fascinated by all the goings-on in the kitchen. And I loved, loved, loved food. Not like picky-eater kids today. In hindsight, I think I had an appreciation for what went into mak-ing a meal. It didn't happen quickly. I never had microwaved or ready-to-eat anything as a child. Everything was homemade. It may sound corny, but I swear I could taste the love. The collards, the red rice, the beans were not only good *for* me, but it was food that felt good *to* me.

I didn't realize it then, but our Geechee culture placed my childhood in a rarefied world. Not until college did I realize that so many young people lived fast lifestyles out of a reality show. Where I came from, sure, I knew kids who

Gullah (also called Geechee) people in the coastal or Lowcountry region of Georgia and South Carolina are descendants of tribes who were enslaved from Central and West Africa. Being on isolated islands and coastal plantations helped them preserve some language and many other elements of Africa, creating a rich and distinctive Gullah culture that endures to the present day.

acted out. But for the most part, we *wanted* to make our families proud. It's a tight-knit world, to this day, that is relatively insular. That's because, probably more than any other community of Black people in this country, we were able to hold on to some of our African flair: elements of the language, food, and more. For example, religion and spirituality weren't just for church-y folks. Obviously, enslaved people were exposed to Christianity. But many of those practices were woven into African systems of belief. Values like God and community, kinship, respect for elders, honoring the ancestors, and a near-sacred connection to nature are part of my DNA.

For as long as I can remember, I've been called an "old soul." And I think my Geechee upbringing is largely the reason why. Those time-honored customs of decorum and formal manners? That's Gullah Geechee, and that's who I am.

But, oh—how my folks have shaped American cuisine. Our enslaved ancestors were given food scraps and damaged crops, and they used what they had access to—which was not much at all. Geechee people had a diet that was primarily local. And don't forget, our communities settled on the shores of the Atlantic. That means lots of seafood and also vegetables, fruits, and of course rice—a significant number of Gullah people came here from the rice-growing regions of West Africa. There were foods imported from Africa during the slave trade, like okra, yams, peas, hot peppers, benne (sesame) seeds, sorghum, and watermelon. Then, of course, let's remember the Indigenous folks who were here long before our arrival: Native Americans introduced good stuff such as corn, squash, tomatoes, and berries.

Some of y'all already know. In Black colloquialism, there's something called "making a dollar outta 15 cent" or "making a way out of no way." Say "amen," somebody! Nowhere in our culture is that spirit of ingenuity more alive than in our rich history of food. As enslaved people, we were given rations—scraps really. And we had to make use of whatever was available.

Maybe that's why you hear Black folks refer to cooking as "fixin' food." We were forced to *fix* what little we had—to fashion some kind of sustenance for our families. But because of who we are, we took it further—making meals not only to feed and strengthen the body but to create sensory experiences to delight the soul. It's what I love most, cousins, about the blessing of Divine Miss Brown coming into your homes.

I feel very strongly that good food—and I'm talking really good food—doesn't have to have a super-fancy lineage. It doesn't need to be expensive. I never get tired of showing people who tune in to watch that it doesn't take much to make a lot. That's why I'm so excited to bring you these recipes, from the heart of my home to yours.

When I saw my mother at the stove, basting and tasting—especially on Sundays—I could sense, even as a little girl, that she was in her element. A medley of sweet and savory smells mixed with the soulful sounds of Anita Baker floating through the house—I felt her peace. Natural-born food lover that I am, I knew Ma's smothered Turkey wings, fried chicken, shrimp and grits, and other dishes—the divine and delicious results of her hours-long meditations—were well worth the wait. I loved to watch and learn. The vibe was super chill. And I instinctively knew to heed the words of one of her favorite jams:

Don't disturb this grooove!

My ma's every move was effortless, like a dance. Not choreographed so much as freestyle. We grew much of what we ate. And like the TV cooking challenges I now host on the Food Network, the ingredients—and ultimately the dishes—depended on the garden pickings of that day. Were the peas ripe for snapping? How was the cabbage looking? If our squash and peppers met her satisfaction, they might end up in her famous pan-fried squash and sausage. As a single mom who often worked two jobs, sometimes three, to make sure I had little extras—the latest sneakers and hairstyles—Ma might allow ya girl to do a lil' sumpin' sumpin', like prep mac and cheese. But that's about it.

I didn't mind. It was during these times that I had Ma all to myself. I am my mother's only child, so it's not as though I ever really wanted for attention, but like most families our weekdays were hurried. With no siblings in the house, I didn't always have a playmate around. Ma and I always spent plenty of time together, but she indulged me a bit with her undivided attention on Sundays in the kitchen. That's when I would sidle up to the Formica counter with my favorite Cabbage Patch doll, Buddy, and his kid sister. She was soft and chubby, with chestnut-colored skin perfectly set off by her blue jumper. We engaged in "deep" conversations about my classmates and the goings-on in the neighborhood, and sometimes Ma would join in, between cooking. Usually, with my tales well within earshot, Ma might sprinkle in some gentle chide like, "I told you, Kardea, not everybody around you is your friend. Don't forget that." But more often than not, as she thought out loud, Ma would make comments about the food she was preparing. Like, "I put my foot in this" or "This is slammin'!" When I heard her utter these words, I just knew I was in for a treat.

The kitchen scene at Grandma's house nearby carried that same spirit: relaxed, cozy, a subtle reverence all wrapped in a warm hug. As a kid, I'd split my time between the two matriarchs, who made sure, with a look or sometimes a backhand, I kept the sense God gave me; and we made a comfortable threesome. *Spoiled* is a loaded word, so let's just say I was well loved. But even as the doted-on first—and for a long while, only—granddaughter, I knew my place. When Grandma said, "Oh, baby, you don't have to help," she wasn't being polite. It was a warm, down-home way of saying: "I don't want nobody in my kitchen." I mean, of course, I could enter the kitchen while Grandma cooked; I just couldn't be *all in there*, up underneath—"Mixing up," in her words.

Family was and *is* central to my soul. I had a small village; there was a simplicity to my life, and my social circle was pretty tight. "Cousins" were my primary entertainment. Not blood relations, but the kids from the families that Ma knew, Grandma knew before her, and probably her mama knew as well.

When you think about it, that's how traditions and culture are made. Right? Of course, as a little girl, I wasn't thinking about these things. Still, I think I did know, on some level, that I was being poured into. And for me, the kitchen, maybe because of the tangible goodness that danced and sang on my tastebuds, was the most memorable impact of those traditions. In the kitchen is where I got to see and hear about all the special ways our families and our way of life went into the way *we* made pound cake, the way *we* prepared Hoppin' John (page 35). It was a feel-good place, where love was poured in and stirred and baked and simmered till even more love came out.

So when I was in Grandma's kitchen, you best believe I was careful to "stay out the way." The last thing I wanted to do was break her rules—even the unwritten ones. Grandma had a way with offhanded comments as she cooked—almost as though she was in a conversation with the food she was preparing. And I was soaking it *all* in.

I had my first chance to put those observation skills to the test when I was about thirteen or fourteen years old. It was a time when I was hanging at my half-sister Evita's house. Somebody—I don't remember who—got the idea that we should cook that night's dinner. I didn't let on that I wasn't allowed to cook by myself at home. I just jumped up all big and bad and boldly said, "I'll make the mac and cheese!"

No one doubted me outright, at least not to my face. But I seem to recall some looks on their faces that read something like, "Um, okay, baby girl—you sure?" The mac and cheese, as part of a traditional Black meal event, is right up there with the ribs or the main dish. I mean, yes, it is technically a side. But its level of importance is really hard to even put into words. I knew I couldn't mess up. I took my time and painstakingly mimicked everything I'd watched Ma and Grandma do.

When I finally took my Pyrex dish out of the oven, the cheeses were bubbling and brimming over the sides. The edges were nicely browned. Once I sat it on the counter, I was grinning from ear to ear because I knew I'd put my whole foot in that mac and cheese. It was *slamming*—and I could tell just by the look of it. When I smelled it, I couldn't help but stick my chest out—with my back a little straighter. I was smelling myself!

I loved every minute. Throughout the process—meticulously shredding and cutting the cheese, whisking the roux, eyeballing the flour just right, folding in two eggs at just the right point (for that authentically southern touch), tenting the foil toward the end of the baking time—ya girl was on point. All the while, my grandmother was in my head. She was always proud of me, always praising my every accomplishment. But this was different. It wasn't a spelling bee or a math test—all important. This was *us*. Our heritage. Our pride. Our family. I so wanted her to see this act of food preparation for all of what it was.

Getting it right not only meant that I could fix a mean dish, that I could cook a lil' sumpin' sumpin'—no, it was deeper than that. I didn't have the words to name it, but nailing the mac and cheese meant that what she'd been steadfastly pouring into me had been received—that I understood the assignment of carrying the torch, becoming the kind of young woman who embodied the spirit of the ancestors.

I knew I didn't have to, yet I so wanted to please her. To be a testament to her legacy.

Grandma had always been my superhero. She was born one of fourteen children on Wadmalaw Island, a stone's throw from Charleston, South Carolina. My grandmother dreamed big. She didn't talk a whole lotta smack, to hear my family tell it. But she had a quiet strength—so much so that while all of her siblings settled nearby, Grandma had the temerity not only to leave the island but to hightail it to New York City of all places. With a degree in nursing and professional aspirations, she left the Lowcountry for the Big Apple.

Who are Gullah and where do they originate from? Here are some interesting statistics to show the ancestry of modern Gullah folks.

FROM 1716 TO 1744:

- 51% of enslaved Black folks brought to Charleston, South Carolina, and later taken to Georgia, came from Angola, which includes present-day Angola and the Congo.
- 7.4% came from Senegambia.
- 4.7% came from the Bight of Biafra, which encompasses most of present-day (coastal) southern Nigeria.
- 2.8% came from the Gold Coast, which is now Ghana.
- 0.2% came from the Windward Coast, which is now Liberia and Côte d'Ivoire.
- 33.9% came from the Caribbean Islands or unknown locations.

FROM 1749 TO 1787:

- 25.2% of enslaved Black people taken to the Sea Islands came from Senegambia.
- 16.7% came from Liberia and Côte d'Ivoire.
- 14.6% came from what is now Angola and Congo.
- 13.1% came from present-day Ghana.
- 6.6% came from Sierra Leone.
- 2.2% came from the Bight of Benin, in what is now Benin and Togo.
- 0.8% came from the Bight of Biafra, now southern Nigeria.
- 20.7% came from the Caribbean Islands.

FROM 1804 TO 1807:

- 52% of the Africans who became Gullah came from Angola and the Congo.
- 17.9% came from Liberia and Côte d'Ivoire.
- 11.4% came from Ghana.
- 4.7% came from Sierra Leone.
- 1.7% came from Senegambia.
- 2.5% came from (coastal) southern Nigeria.
- 1.6% came from Madagascar and Mozambique.
- 8.2% came from the Caribbean Islands.

Source: Elizabeth Donnan, ed., *Documents Illustrative of the History of the Slave Trade to America,* vol. 4 (Washington, DC: Carnegie Institution of Washington, 1935).

Grandma may have left Gullah for New York City, but Gullah never left her. It was in her kitchen that the culture and traditions were brought to life for me at a very young age. She taught me everything she had taught my mom and everything her mom had taught her as a little girl. It's always been so important that Gullah—the language, yes, but especially the food—was honored, revered even. Think about it. As enslaved people, Black folks weren't allowed to learn to read or write, so we really had to be creative and come up with ways to hold on to our truth as a people.

She showed me how to make grits, lima beans, and okra stew. But it wasn't just about boiling, frying, and adding a little this and that. Grandma made sure I knew the "why" behind the foods she prepared. For example, on Fridays okra stew—a big ole pot—was a kind of feast at the end of a long workweek. It was when folks came back to the island from laboring for white people in the city.

When Grandma spoke, I hung on her every syllable. She didn't waste words; everything she said was thoughtful. More often than not she would remind me of how fortunate I was, "Don't forget to thank the Good Lord for everything in your life; you are blessed my child." My grandmother always stressed taking your time and listening with the intention of understanding. She never rushed anything. She always handled things with care and grace. Including cooking.

GOD'S PLAN

I always enjoyed watching cooking shows in much the same way as some people like to watch soap operas. Pure entertainment. Even if you know a nurse, like Grandma, you never see yourself in the characters or plotlines of *General Hospital*. Right?

When Emeril Lagasse yelled, *"BAM!"* I was as tickled as millions of other people sitting in front of the TV. What he was doing was about as real to me as Luke and Laura dying and coming back to life. Trust and believe—I did not see *Delicious Miss Brown* or the Food Network anywhere in my future.

Ma encouraged me to go to college and pursue a solid professional life. It's the life she worked hard to provide for me. Education was very important in my house. So as a young adult, I did just that. I had a ton of enthusiasm and a heart for justice. With a bachelor's degree and dreams to change the world, I got a job as a social worker. It seemed the perfect fit because I always loved children. My role in a state placement agency put me in charge of children's well-being. I was sometimes taking kids from bad environments and finding safe homes for them. Then I'd track their progress, as well as their birth parents'. The goal, of course, was to reunite families and make sure kids were cared for and set up for success.

I loved the idea of helping people. It's how I was raised—with a "village." I know people like to talk about community. But in Gullah Geechee culture, we live it. There was no one at church, in our neighborhood, or in our circle whose needs were not met by nearby family members. Whether it meant bringing over a hot plate if someone became ill or taking up a collection if someone experienced a loss in the family—where I come from, folks rallied. When Ma had to work late, if Grandma's job kept her from looking after me, there were always "aunties" and "cousins" and friends down the street. Growing up, all of my friends had that same kind of support. At the time, it never dawned on me that this was rooted in our Gullah-centered traditions. And to me, it was just plain wrong that there were kids out there with absolutely no one to look after them. I saw my career as a way to give back and make sure no child had to do without the kind of love and attention that nurtured me.

Fueled by passion and idealistic visions of peace and joy dancing in my head, I poured every ounce of my twenty-something-year-old energy into social work. It felt so gratifying to break into my career. I felt as though I was doing everything "right"—college, career, advanced degree—that things were going the way they were supposed to.

Until they weren't.

I discovered that oftentimes I couldn't make a difference in a child's life, or not the difference I wanted. My heart was in it, but the needs were far too great for me—or even for a child-protection agency—to address. Parents who were abusive or dealing with substance addiction did not always manage to change those patterns. Other times, the "safe" spaces the system placed children in turned out to be just as awful, if not worse. I wanted to bring families together, not upend lives.

It was 2012. I was a year out of college. And cousins, ya girl was burned out—fried. And the thing about it is, I didn't really realize how much I had on me. And then things started tumbling down. My body started turning on me. I'd always carried my tension and worry in my neck and shoulders. But my head began to ache almost constantly—my back hurt to the point where I could barely stand to sit at my desk. Then came the panic attacks.

Now, *that* was scary.

Cousins, I don't know who all needs to hear this: I'm not talking about a little nervousness. A panic attack can feel like full-on cardiac arrest. If you've never experienced one, I pray you never do. It's as though, in an outer-body type experience, you are confronting the most frightening thing imaginable, like falling from a bridge or racing from a burning building. Now, we all know that mental health is not something we deal with well in American society. And in the Black community, the subject is more than a pink elephant. Many people see mental health struggles as a sign of weakness—something only privileged people, who have the luxury of halting their grind to "dwell" on things, experience. Often we've heard words like, "I'm too blessed to be stressed." And I think too many of us have internalized the idea that "ain't nobody got time" for depression. As unfortunate and damaging as that thinking may be, it does make sense in a certain context.

Yes, I know I am from a line of Strong Women. I will proudly carry that mantle, but not at the cost of my peace and well-being. Growing up, the closest we came to talking about anxiety and depression was coded and spoken in ominous whispers. Occasionally, I would learn that so-and-so "had a case of bad nerves." What that meant exactly was anybody's guess. I was not prepared for the emotional anguish I was going through. It had no vocabulary. I did know I needed help.

I knew it wasn't going to be easy to explain—that Ma and Grandma might not understand what I was going through. I didn't expect my family to "get it." I just always knew that whatever "it" was, they would love me through it. I can still remember one time, after a horrible panic attack—crying, praying, and trying to figure out what to do with myself—I barely recognized the body I was in. It was racked with pain, not functioning properly. I couldn't even swallow food. And I could almost hear my grandma's voice saying, "What you're NOT about to do is sit up somewhere by yourself."

I could no longer work. I lost my apartment after struggling quietly for months to make ends meet on disability checks. I moved back home. Blessedly, I come from a people who love Jesus—a family of strong believers in James 2:26: faith without works is dead. So, yes, they prayed with me. But they also carried me to a psychiatrist. The diagnosis? Generalized anxiety disorder. And as I knew all along, it was *not* all in my head.

I did everything the doctor ordered—went to weekly therapy sessions, took my medicine, and practiced stress-relief rituals like breathwork. To this day, I believe the key to the success I enjoy right now can be traced back to a quiet conversation I had with my aunt Sharon. We talked and cried together about my mental health crisis for a really long while one evening. After listening to me carefully, never doubtful or judgmental, she spoke seven words I will never forget: "God is trying to tell you something."

I get chills thinking about it even today. It's not as though I discovered that very night what God was saying to me in the midst of all my struggles. But it was the powerful reminder I needed to affirm that I was not broken or damaged. What I was going through was simply God's way of course correction. Old folks always say that first comes the test—then the testimony. So here I was in the thick of the most difficult test of my young life. But hearing those words from Auntie let me know there was a blessing on the other side. Not gonna lie—I had no idea what it looked like, but I was reminded that night that faith would bring me through.

Auntie wasn't done showing me the way that night. She introduced me to a whole host of spiritual practices that opened my eyes, although I'd been a Christian my entire life and grew up in the church. Some of her thinking might be considered New Age-y or "out there." But here's what I know: God is real. And anything you do to get closer to Him? Cousins, I'm here to tell you—it's rewarded.

If I haven't already made it clear, I need to say it louder for the folks in the back. Y'all, I was on a mission. I knew I had to get right in my spirit *and* in my mind. One without the other was not going to get me where I needed to be. After some months in my wellness journey, I was led to simply ask God, "Why?" Not everyone understands that at first. A lot of times we want to ask God why—as in, "Why me?"

I come from a very special place—even when I was too young or naive to articulate it, I always knew that being close to the land, close to family and community, and close to the Word gave me comfort. It gave me a certain confidence too, a sureness about who I was and how much I mattered, not as someone fancy or entitled—but as someone who is His child. I didn't need to know why. I know His ways are far higher than my ways. So I couldn't imagine even fixing my mouth for that. I needed to know what God wanted me to do.

As sure as you're sitting down with this book right now, I heard the Lord say, "Move." And so I did.

Ma gave me her full support but didn't understand it at first. I'm not sure I did either, actually. But I had visited my cousin in New Jersey about a year prior to having my "relocate" conversation with God. On God's instruction to move, I figured the Garden State, as they call it, was where he aimed for me to go. Don't laugh. I know it's not the

most glamorous locale a girl could choose. Most folks probably get "called" to California or New York—the kinds of places where dreams are made.

Cousins, please understand, this wasn't about dreaming. It was about *destiny*. Somewhere deep inside I just felt that. I don't know how or why. Maybe I simply needed to leave the nest, and this transition felt best. I was certain that after getting back to me, I needed to get out of my comfort zone. My family had been loving on me—well, all my life, of course—but especially hard during a very difficult time. Now, I had to test my wings.

GET ON UP

One thing about me: I'm always going to lead with my heart. The move to New Jersey didn't change that. I landed a promising role with Big Brothers Big Sisters of America—a great opportunity for the social worker in me to help children, but in a high-level, more structured way by creating mentorship programs. My home base was in a lovely and sophisticated suburb, only about ten miles from Manhattan. I had the best of both worlds: a chance to live like a city slicker, riding the subway to midtown, where I got a taste for the fast life; and then retreat to a warm community with a semblance of small-town values.

Life wasn't totally Pleasantville, USA, despite the lovely surroundings, though. I was staying with a relative when I first moved up north. And my goal was to room with them until I'd saved enough money to get my own place. But things took a turn soon after I arrived. I was, and still remain, grateful for the kindness and support of extended family. But before long, it so happened that the living arrangements didn't quite work out. It seemed best that I make the difficult decision to find another spot. With no place to go, I packed my car with the little belongings I came with and headed to a low-cost hotel for as long as my pennies would allow. I ended up staying between two friends—one a coworker in Newark; the other a friend in Brooklyn, traveling back and forth to New Jersey for work. It was wild, y'all.

I was essentially homeless, with about a month's pay saved up. At one point I was able to rent an apartment in a two-family house. Then the owners sold the place without telling me! It was one of those feet-don't-fail-me-now times that I can look back on as one of many defining moments in life. In fact, in retrospect, it's almost funny when I think about all the doors that *seemed* to be closing.

Throughout all the crazy, I had been dating a special person. And eventually we settled into a committed relationship and moved in together. Our place was a modest size and ideally located for the commute to my office in Newark. And it was fun to have a steady boo. Before he and I got together, New Jersey living hadn't presented many chances for me to cook the way I was used to. In my boyfriend I had a steady taste tester with a man-size appetite—a great opportunity to practice my Lowcountry Gullah recipes and invent new ones.

Importantly, cooking also helped me decompress. Yes, I was in a pretty good place mentally. God watches over His, so it was no coincidence that one of the first work friends I met in New Jersey was this amazing woman who, initially, intimidated me. I wasn't accustomed to that New York/New Jersey directness. What I mistook as mean was actually a forthright, no-nonsense energy that I loved. Dawn was my oracle, a certified Reiki practitioner. And she'd lay her hands on my head and help me get in touch with energy. To this day, I know that God's hand was all up in that "chance" meeting.

Still, I was acutely aware of the need to look out for myself, to keep anxiety at bay. Self-care had become a part of my life—not on Sundays, or rare occasions, but on the regular. The kitchen was my safe space—just as, in hindsight, I'd witnessed it as the comfort zone for Ma and Grandma before her. I could get lost there, cousins—in a good way—with my tunes blasting, my sauces saucing, and joy flowing.

Cousins, sometimes you have to get out of the way. And let God be God. As it turns out, my Garden State bae was doing more than filling his belly during our time together. He was watching me in the kitchen—taking note of the food and the feeling that came out with the pork chops, gravy, and pound cake. Without so much as a whisper from me, he took a video of me cooking. Without my knowledge he submitted the video of me cooking in the kitchen to a casting call on cookingchannel.com. The casting call was for homecooks across America to be featured on a new traveling cooking show.

Cousins, the network suits picked me!

Out of hundreds of submissions, mine was chosen to be featured on the pilot of a new show called *Deen of Lean*. The host, Bobby Deen, was tapped to feature healthier versions of his mom's signature southern dishes.

I am a South Carolinian whose go-to dishes are based on southern traditions. I was to cook alongside Bobby in hopes the public would warm to the idea of classic comfort southern dishes, prepared with less decadence and fewer calories. The Cooking Channel sent a film crew to my New Jersey cul-de-sac with a trailer—the works. Let me remind y'all: I had never been on TV. I had never cooked in front of cameras (unless we count my smartphone). And I had never seen, never even been near, a television set, crew, or makeup team.

Now cousins, you may be wondering—I get asked this question all the time— "Kardea, weren't you nervous?" Or another one people want to know: "What did you do to prepare?" Two words, y'all—*no* and *nothing*. Of course I was excited about the amazing opportunity. But someone directing me to cook on TV was akin to someone telling me to breathe while I walk. What was there to fret? Where did practice come into doing something so natural?

My biggest concern was what I'd wear; I wasn't stressed out, though—more like the nice tingle of excitement of preparing for a first date. And even that was mitigated by my bank account. Social work doesn't really pay well, so there weren't a ton of options for me to consider, really. I needed to ball on a budget, so I stepped up in Easy Pickins, an affordable chain throughout New Jersey where the fashion assortment was just as the name says—easy on the wallet. I picked up a lil' blue top to match the African head wrap I planned to swathe over my cropped natural 'do. And nothing I've ever done has felt so effortless. I was comfortable chopping, cooking, talking, laughing. Storytelling is in every fiber of my being, so I never ran out of food and family folklore to share. There was literally not a whisper of tension. No concern, no edge. In no way did I feel skittish. It was as though I was entirely free.

The first thing I did once filming wrapped was call home. I was crying so hard I could barely get the words out. I said, "Ma, they want me to do this—for real, for real." Grandma was like, "Do what? Make mac and cheese? What kind of sense does that make?" They both felt the spirit behind my words, I think. The ease, the peace. And they recognized what it meant to me. Doing *my* thing.

Whenever I tell this story, right about now is where I have to stop. And. Just. Breathe. I can't help it because here is the point when my whole life began to change. About eight months later, I quit my job because it was so clear that God had given me my assignment. Y'all, I found my purpose on that day—what I was put here to do was revealed to me. The whole time He'd been working things out for my good. So this is where I *must* take a minute and say, "Thank you, God! Thank you for everything. The bumps, the pain, the tears—EV-ER-Y-THING!"

IMMA GET ON THIS TV, MA

Cousins, I was not suddenly catapulted onto your TV screens after filming *Deen of Lean*. The pilot was not picked up. But the producers really loved me and wanted to do more with me. They wanted to pitch me as a talent for my VERY OWN show.

For sure, during the pilot shoot all the pieces to the puzzle seemed to click. I enjoyed working with the crew and nothing else in my life ever felt this right. Pat (the producer) took me to several pitches at Food Network's headquarters in New York City. The feedback from the TV executives was great. Still, there was a "but" at the end of all their praise:

- *"But you're too green . . ."*
- *"But you're not a classically trained chef . . ."*
- *"But you have no experience in the food industry . . ."*
- *"But we don't think you're ready to host your own show . . ."*
- *"But you're _____"* (Fill in the blank, chile!)

I soon learned something I guess I could've gleaned as even a passive consumer of popular culture—which is how few spaces in society exist for people who look like me. Not many spaces for women. Fewer still for women who look like me.

As much as I love food, and always have—as much as I love eating, preparing food, and feeding people I love—the truth is, it wasn't enough.

Once I put my lil' feelings on a shelf, it was clear that the network folks had constructive criticism that I needed to take note of. There were a few people I met and developed friendships with who were rooting for me at the network. And through a series of ad hoc guest spots on Food Network shows, I learned a lot by watching other hosts. Fortunately, I don't have the spirit of a wallower. You know that "woe is me" victim energy? I let myself sulk for a short while. And then I realized I had to get to gettin'—like the old country folks say.

What came next may surprise you: I left New Jersey. Yes, I was beyond confident about what God had planned for my life, but sitting around waiting for other people to come around was not the way. Remember, I was raised in The Church. I'm all about Faith + Works. Cousins, I knew I had to make things happen, and I knew I needed the kind of support only family could provide. I realized that in order for TV executives to take me seriously, I needed to take me seriously—with some skin in the game.

The fact is, there was a lot I didn't know. Ma, Grandma—no one in our family cooked like the people on television. We didn't use gadgets and tools, like peelers. We didn't measure. And when we cooked for our family, we just cooked plenty to eat. We didn't break down recipes into serving sizes. Gullah cooking is all about tradition and intuition. People who watch cooking shows want and need something they can actually do: practical instruction.

I don't think it's just me, but I find that God doesn't let anything go to waste. Know what I mean? Months before I headed back home—in fact, I was still working my nine-to-five at the time—I was on my way back to the house after a really long day. As usual, I found myself thinking, hoping, and praying about how I was going to leave social work for television. That day I got a call from someone in the industry just as I was staring out the window talking to God. He too knew I had to learn. And he told me about a new San Francisco–based pop-up called Feastly that was doing really creative things and gaining widespread attention. It piqued my interest, and I kept it in the back of my mind for a long time. I knew then it was a great idea, but if I were to do anything similar, it needed to be on a much smaller scale and have some kind of Kardea seasoning sprinkled on top for it to be authentic.

Once I moved back home, of course, I had to support myself. I got a job as a driver for a catering company, making $7.25 an hour. Me being me, I didn't just drive. I was all up in the kitchen and everything—trying to soak in knowledge. I soon decided to launch a Kardea version of catering—something on-brand and on-purpose: traveling New Gullah Supper Club pop-ups.

The idea was "let me bring the Lowcountry experience to you!" Now ya girl had no capital, no backers, no nothing, really, that would make something like this make sense. Oh, and did I mention that I'd lost my car? Yeah, I was having more than a few financial setbacks. But I had faith—decided I could feel bad about my setbacks or look at them as a setup for better things. After all, I know that when God puts something on your heart, there is no turning back.

Can't say I had a business plan, exactly. But at the time I did have about a thousand followers on the 'Gram. So I figured they could be my marketing base. My Auntie Lisa bought me some plates and whatnot. And I raised nearly $2,000 with a GoFundMe effort. In 2015, I got a great turnout in Atlanta for what I called a soft launch, a mixer of sorts—mostly because I didn't yet have the funds to go all out on pricey ingredients.

My New Gullah Supper Club made up for any lack by packing in a whole lot of flavor— with help, of course. I did all of the cooking. But my mom, Aunt TC (for "Too Cute"), and lots of friends and family served. My godbrother, Donnovan Jones, would sing— make that *sang*. My boy could blow! Together we'd hit two or three cities a month in and around the Charleston-Atlanta corridor. Over time, the supper club pop-ups really caught on—with ads, spirits sponsorships, and coverage in the local press. We were doing girls' trips, bachelor parties—you name it. People were bringing me on as a private chef for large parties. I'd even coordinate themed drinks. One consistent crowd-pleaser was Swamp Water (page 270), which was basically spiked sweet tea, lemonade, and ginger beer.

Meanwhile, I was still driving for the corporate catering company, learning as much about the business as possible, and discreetly letting the businesspeople know they should consider the New Gullah Supper Club for their social events. A year passed, then another and another. All this time, my dream of hosting a food show was my North Star. But I gotta tell you, I was digging my success with the supper club. And I was proud that word was spreading about my specialties, like pimento cheese–buttered crostini and Sweet Potato Cheesecake (page 88).

Fortunately, over the course of several years, the success I was having with my New Gullah Supper Club served to enhance my profile on social media as well as in traditional media. The Food Network continued to book me for occasional guest appearances on some of its popular shows—including *BBQ Blitz*, *Farmhouse Rules*, and *Cooks vs. Cons*.

Four years after I first stood in front of a camera to cook up a little something on an otherwise unremarkable day in 2018, God showed up and showed up. I was out on a delivery for the catering company when I heard from Pat (the producer from *Deen of Lean*) with whom I'd become friendly. He said the market was really hot and wanted to take a stab at pitching me to Food Network one more time. Mind you three years had passed since the original pitch. I received another call a few weeks later from Pat; the network had finally said YES. They ordered a proof of concept and wanted it to be filmed right way! A proof of concept is a more condensed version of a pilot. With ya girl as host—not a guest host, not a judge—a show to be shot on Edisto Island and centered on *my* home cooking, *my* family! Cousins, I don't know where you're reading this book right now. But if you experienced anything like thunder and lightning in that moment—it was me, shouting and giving Him thanks with the wildest praise dance you've ever seen!

As I write this, *Delicious Miss Brown* is entering its seventh season—that's close to one hundred shows, and so many scrumptious dishes—including Deviled Crabs (page 67), Lowcountry Boil (page 40), and Sweet Potato Pone (page 77). By far the most amazing and beautiful part of the journey so far has been *you*! The love from long-time viewers, Instagram followers, and Facebook friends—even people discovering *Delicious Miss Brown* for the first time—continues to warm my heart and feed my soul. Please trust and believe the feeling is mutual.

Y'all are family now—and you're stuck with me! I wrote this cookbook out of that love. It is not my cookbook; it's ours, born out of our deep and abiding connection. I want the recipes on these pages, this food, to fill you up. Each and every dish is a part of me—from crowd favorites like Red Rice (page 39), Aunt TC's Lemon-Lime Soda Cake (page 93), and Country Potato Salad (page 55) to my hearty one-pot dishes like Snookums's Okra Soup (page 51) and Smoked Sausage and Egg Skillet (page 143).

New Gullah

Can I just tell you, cousins,

I am so, so blessed. If I had to point to one part of this amazing journey—believe me, sometimes I swear I have to pinch myself, it overwhelms my spirit to be welcomed into your home every week. But what I love most is sharing with you. I was always that kid who wanted to make her mama and her whole family proud. So I'm honored to be pleasing the ancestors by bringing a little bit of Gullah Geechee into your life. It means everything to me—not only to bring it, but to see how warmly you receive it. You already know that Gullah people have been able to hold on to African names, African folktales, and so much more. The Sea Islands are a very special place, an area where enslaved West Africans were brought to the United States and formed what's known as Gullah. During the seventeenth, eighteenth, and nineteenth centuries, Senegalese, Gambians, and Angolans lived in small farming and fishing communities along the Atlantic coastal plain and the chain of islands that run parallel to it. I could not be prouder of my Gullah Geechee heritage.

But I have to admit, when I was growing up in and around Wadmalaw Island, I took it for granted. The way we spoke, that melodic Creole language, which rose largely out of necessity so that the white slave owners couldn't understand it; the food—delicacies to me, but created from whatever scraps were thrown to my ancestors—I assumed everyone enjoyed the same rich, beautiful way of life. It wasn't until I went away to college that I realized I had a special family background. Folks were tickled by the way I spoke and the stories I shared about our food. And some of the ways they grew up were funny and strange to me too. Not in a bad way, though.

Ma taught me to appreciate all kinds of foods. So learning about different customs and flavors just made me that much more curious. That's one of the reasons I call my cooking *New* Gullah—as in my own personal interpretation of the traditions that make up classic Gullah cooking. I've always loved experimenting. Back when I was growing up, I'd take the foods Ma and Grandma had fixed for me and play with different flavors here and there. What can I tell you, cousins? Ya girl likes to play and mix things up a bit.

When I get ready to make my Buffalo Blue Fried Shrimp (page 48), cousins, I know good and well the ancestors weren't hardly sprinkling blue cheese crumbles on classic soul food. But here we are! It's fun, it's delicious, and it's a modern twist. When I add a lil' sumpin' sumpin', it's always to honor and pay homage, not bastardize, Gullah culture. After all, I am rooted in this food. It's all a part of who I am.

If you were to experience the New Gullah Supper Club, you'd get a full sensory immersion—music, storytelling, drinks, starters, sides, entrees, dessert—because our Gullah Geechee traditions can't be distilled into one thing. The culture is too rich, too extensive. And it lives in me and all Gullah descendants. So please know that when I share the foods I grew up with, you are getting a very special piece of me.

Miss Brown's House Seasoning

My house seasoning can be used on nearly everything. Especially poultry, vegetables, seafood, red meat, and so much more! You'll see the seasoning used in recipes like Chicken Perloo (page 43), Fried Oysters (page 47), Fried Grits Balls with Tasso Ham (page 127), and Slow-Cooked Brisket Sloppy Joes with Frizzled Onions (page 202), to name a few. I store my house seasoning in an airtight glass container in a dark, cool space.

1 teaspoon onion powder

1 teaspoon kosher salt

1 teaspoon freshly ground black pepper

1 teaspoon sweet paprika

1 teaspoon garlic powder

In a small bowl, combine the onion powder, salt, pepper, paprika, and garlic powder. You can make as much seasoning as you want, using multiple teaspoons of each until you reach the desired quantity. It can be stored in an airtight container for up to one year.

Hoppin' John

This dish dates back centuries in the Lowcountry. It was introduced by West African enslaved people in the coastal regions of the south. Slaves would make large pots of rice with beans to hold them over while they worked in the fields. As time progressed, the meal became a symbol of wealth on New Year's Day.

Serves 4 to 6

2 cups dried field peas, rinsed

1 small piece smoked turkey neck or ham hock

Kosher salt

4 tablespoons (½ stick) unsalted butter, divided

1 tablespoon vegetable oil

1 medium onion, diced into 1/2-inch pieces

1 small green bell pepper, diced into 1/2-inch pieces

Freshly ground black pepper

2 cloves garlic, minced

2 cups long-grain white rice

2 scallions, sliced

Heat a medium heavy-bottomed saucepot or Dutch oven over medium-high heat. Add the field peas and cover with cold water by 1 inch (should be about 6 cups water). Add the smoked turkey and a few generous pinches of salt and bring to a boil. Reduce to a simmer, cover, and cook over medium heat until tender, about 2 hours, then turn off the heat. Do not drain.

Melt 2 tablespoons of the butter in a large saucepot over medium-high heat and add the oil. Add the onion and green pepper. Season with salt and pepper and cook just until slightly softened, about 5 minutes. Add the garlic and cook 1 minute more. Add the rice to the pot and cook, stirring, until toasted, about 5 minutes.

Add 3 cups water and 1 cup of the cooking liquid from the peas. Bring to a boil, then cover and cook over medium-low heat until the rice is tender and cooked through, 15 to 20 minutes. Fluff the rice with a fork and gently stir in the cooked peas, drained, and the remaining 2 tablespoons of butter. Cover and cook for 10 minutes more. Transfer to a serving bowl and top with the sliced scallions before serving.

Limpin' Susan

3 slices thick-cut bacon, cut into 1-inch pieces

2 pounds medium shrimp, peeled and deveined

2 tablespoons unsalted butter

3 tablespoons vegetable oil

1 yellow onion, diced

2 cloves garlic, minced

2 cups sliced fresh or thawed frozen okra

1 teaspoon freshly squeezed lemon juice

1 cup long-grain white rice

2 cups chicken stock

1 teaspoon kosher salt

½ teaspoon freshly ground black pepper

In a heavy-bottomed skillet (preferably cast-iron), cook the bacon over medium heat until crisp, 5 to 7 minutes. Remove the bacon and drain on paper towels. Add the shrimp to the bacon fat and cook until just barely seared, about 4 minutes. Remove to a separate plate. Melt the butter in the skillet over medium heat and add the oil. Stir in the onion and garlic. Cook until the onion is starting to soften, 2 to 3 minutes, then add the okra and cook for 5 minutes. Stir in the lemon juice (this will help cut the slime) and the rice. Sauté until the onion is lightly browned, about 3 minutes more. Add the chicken stock, salt, and pepper and bring to a boil over high heat, stirring to loosen any browned bits on the bottom of the skillet. Reduce the heat to low and return the shrimp to the skillet. Cover and cook until the rice is tender and cooked through, about 20 minutes. During the last 5 minutes of cooking time, use a fork to stir the bacon into the rice. Fluff and serve.

Red Rice

2 cups parboiled rice

¼ cup vegetable oil

8 ounces smoked pork sausage, finely diced

1 large onion, finely diced

1 green bell pepper, finely diced

2 6-ounce cans tomato paste

4 teaspoons sugar

1 tablespoon garlic powder

1 tablespoon kosher salt

1 tablespoon freshly ground black pepper

Rinse the rice until the water runs slightly clear. (This removes the starch.)

Preheat the oven to 350°F. In a large frying pan, heat the oil over medium-high heat. Add the sausage, onion, and pepper and cook, stirring, until the vegetables soften and start to brown at the edges, 3 to 4 minutes. Stir in the tomato paste, sugar, garlic powder, salt, and pepper. Stir the rice into the tomato mixture and cook uncovered, stirring occasionally, about 5 minutes.

Transfer to a 9 × 13-inch or 3-quart baking dish and spread into an even layer. Add just enough water to cover the rice (about 2 cups). Tightly cover with a lid or foil and bake for 30 minutes. Turn off the oven, fluff the rice, cover again, and return to the oven for 10 minutes more.

Lowcountry Boil

2 to 3 tablespoons seafood seasoning, such as Old Bay, or to taste

3 pounds new potatoes, washed

2 16-ounce packages cooked kielbasa sausage, cut into 1-inch pieces

8 ears fresh corn, shucked and cut into halves or thirds

4 pounds fresh blue crabs

4 pounds large fresh shrimp, shells on

Heat a large pot of water over medium-high heat indoors or outside. Add the seafood seasoning to taste and bring to a boil. Add the potatoes and sausage and cook until the potatoes are fork-tender, about 10 minutes. Add the corn and cook until done, about 5 more minutes. Add the crab and cook another 5 minutes. Add the shrimp and cook until they turn pink, 3 to 4 minutes. Sprinkle with additional seafood seasoning before serving.

NOTE: *Reduce measurements by half for smaller serving size.*

Chicken Perloo

5 slices thick-cut bacon, cut into ½-inch pieces

1 small fryer chicken, cut into frying pieces

2 teaspoons Miss Brown's House Seasoning (page 33), or to taste

8 ounces smoked sausage, such as kielbasa or andouille, cut into half moons

1 stalk celery, diced

1 medium Vidalia onion, diced

1 green bell pepper, diced

4 cloves garlic, minced

½ cup dry sherry

3 cups diced ripe tomatoes (beefsteak or heirloom if in season, plum if not)

2 cups long-grain white rice, such as Carolina Gold Rice

2 tablespoons unsalted butter

4 cups (1 quart) chicken stock

¼ cup chopped fresh curly-leaf parsley, for serving (optional)

Heat a large heavy-bottomed skillet or Dutch oven over medium heat. Add the bacon and cook, stirring occasionally, until the bacon is crisp and the fat is rendered, 3 to 4 minutes. Using a slotted spoon, transfer the bacon to a paper towel–lined plate, leaving the rendered fat in the pan.

Sprinkle both sides of the chicken with the House Seasoning. Increase the heat to medium-high and add the chicken, skin-side down, and the sausage to the skillet. Sear the chicken on one side, stirring and flipping the sausage occasionally, until the chicken is deep golden brown, 4 to 5 minutes. Flip the chicken and cook for another 3 to 4 minutes on the other side. Remove the chicken and sausage to a plate.

Add the celery, onion, and pepper to the remaining bacon and chicken fat in the skillet. Cook until the vegetables are softened and starting to brown, about 5 minutes. Add the garlic and cook, stirring, for 1 minute. Pour in the sherry and use a wooden spoon to scrape the browned bits from the bottom of the skillet. Stir in the tomatoes and cook until they release all their juices, 3 to 4 minutes. Stir in the rice and butter and cook for about 1 minute. Stir the cooked bacon and sausage back into the skillet. Stir in the chicken stock and add more House Seasoning to taste. Nestle the chicken pieces, skin-side up, back into the pan, adding any juices from the plate.

Bring to a boil, then reduce the heat to low and cover. Simmer until all the liquid is absorbed and the rice is fully cooked, 20 to 30 minutes. Fluff the rice with a fork and sprinkle with parsley, if using. Serve immediately.

Geechee Salsa

¼ cup red wine vinegar

1 tablespoon sugar

½ teaspoon dried oregano

2 or 3 dashes hot sauce

½ cup vegetable oil

2 15.5-ounce cans black-eyed peas, rinsed and drained

1 cup fresh or thawed frozen corn kernels

1 small red onion, finely diced

1 green bell pepper, finely diced

1 4-ounce jar diced pimentos, drained

1 bunch of fresh cilantro, chopped

2 cloves garlic, minced

Kosher salt

Freshly ground black pepper

Whisk together the vinegar, sugar, oregano, and hot sauce in a large bowl. Drizzle in the oil while whisking. Add the peas, corn, onion, bell pepper, pimentos, cilantro, and garlic to the dressing; season with salt and pepper. Toss until everything is coated. The salad can be served immediately, but it's better if it sits refrigerated for a few hours or overnight.

Fried Oysters

1 cup buttermilk

1 cup cornmeal

1 cup all-purpose flour

1 tablespoon Miss Brown's House Seasoning (page 33)

2 cups oysters, freshly shucked or canned, drained

4 cups vegetable oil, for frying

Kosher salt

Freshly ground black pepper

Tartar sauce (optional)

Lemon wedges (optional)

Line a baking sheet with butcher paper or parchment paper. Pour the buttermilk in a bowl.

In another bowl, mix together the cornmeal, the flour, and House Seasoning. Transfer the mixture to a clean paper lunch bag.

Dip the oysters one by one in the buttermilk, then dredge in the flour mixture, shaking the bag to coat. Shake off the excess flour and place the oysters on the prepared baking sheet.

In a Dutch oven or heavy pan, heat the oil to 350°F. Line a baking sheet with paper towels and set a wire rack on top.

Fry half the oysters until golden brown, 1 to 2 minutes per side. Remove to the prepared wire rack to drain. Repeat with the remaining oysters. Sprinkle with a little salt and pepper. Serve hot with tartar sauce and lemon wedges, if using.

Buffalo Blue Fried Shrimp

Serves 4

¾ cup hot sauce

1 tablespoon Worcestershire sauce

3 tablespoons unsalted butter

1 teaspoon garlic powder

½ teaspoon kosher salt

1 teaspoon freshly ground black pepper

1 cup buttermilk

2 cups all-purpose flour

1 ½ tablespoons Miss Brown's House Seasoning (page 33)

1 pound jumbo shrimp, peeled and deveined

4 cups canola oil

Blue cheese crumbles

In a small saucepan, combine the hot sauce, Worcestershire sauce, butter, garlic powder, salt, and pepper. Bring the buffalo sauce to a boil, then reduce to low until ready to serve.

Line a baking sheet with butcher paper or parchment paper. Pour the buttermilk in a bowl.

In another bowl, mix the flour and House Seasoning. Transfer the flour mixture to a clean paper lunch bag.

Dip the shrimp in the buttermilk, then dredge in the flour mixture, shaking the bag to coat. Shake off the excess flour and place the shrimp on the prepared baking sheet.

In a Dutch oven or heavy pan, heat the oil to 350°F. Line a baking sheet with paper towels and set a wire rack on top.

Fry half the shrimp until golden brown, 1 to 2 minutes per side. Remove to the prepared wire rack to drain. Repeat with the remaining shrimp. In a large bowl, toss the fried shrimp with the buffalo sauce. Arrange on a platter and top with crumbled blue cheese.

Snookums's Okra Soup

Snookums was the nickname given to my great-grandfather.

Serves 4 to 6

---

2 tablespoons olive oil

1 large onion, chopped

1 medium green bell pepper, chopped

2 cloves garlic, minced

2 cups fresh or thawed frozen corn

2 cups thawed frozen lima beans

1 cup diced fresh Roma tomatoes

1 28-ounce can diced tomatoes

4 cups vegetable broth

Kosher salt

Freshly ground black pepper

2 tablespoons unsalted butter

2 ½ cups sliced fresh or thawed frozen okra
(if using fresh, slice into 1-inch pieces)

1 teaspoon ground ginger

½ lemon

Steamed rice, for serving (optional)

Heat a large gumbo pot or Dutch oven over medium-high heat. Add the oil, onion, bell pepper, and garlic and sauté until the vegetables soften. Mix in the corn, lima beans, and Roma tomatoes. Add the canned tomatoes, vegetable broth, and a generous pinch of salt and pepper and stir. Turn down heat to a simmer, covered, for about 20 minutes.

In another saucepan over medium-high heat, melt the butter. Add the sliced okra and ginger, season with a little salt and pepper, and stir. Squeeze the half lemon over the okra (the lemon juice will help cut some of the slime). Sauté, stirring occasionally, for 3 to 4 minutes. Turn off the heat.

Once the broth mixture has simmered for 20 minutes, add the okra. Taste and add salt and pepper if needed. Cover and cook for an additional 10 minutes. Stir the soup then serve over rice (or enjoy it without rice).

Sea Island Collard Greens

4 tablespoons (½ stick) unsalted butter

1 tablespoon olive oil

1 extra-large onion, chopped

3 cloves garlic, finely chopped

1 pound smoked turkey (neck, legs, or tail)

2 quarts chicken stock, plus more if needed

1 cup water

3 large bunches (2 pounds) of collard greens with stems, chopped

2 teaspoons sugar

Kosher salt

Freshly ground black pepper

Hot sauce, for serving

In a large, deep pot over medium heat, melt the butter and stir in the oil. Add the onion and sauté until slightly softened, 2 to 3 minutes, then add the garlic and cook for 2 minutes more. Add the turkey, stock, and water to the pot, bring to a boil, then turn down the heat to a simmer. Cook for one hour with the lid on, then add the collard greens in batches, stirring and adding more as they wilt. Stir in the sugar and season with salt and pepper. Simmer with the lid on for an additional hour. Stir, adding more stock if necessary, and continue to cook until the greens are tender, about 20 more minutes. Taste the greens and add salt and pepper if desired. Remove the smoked meat from the bone and add it back to the pot. Serve with a slotted spoon and drizzle with hot sauce.

Country Potato Salad

3 pounds russet potatoes

1 ½ cups mayonnaise, plus more if needed

⅔ cup sweet salad cubes or relish

½ cup yellow mustard

½ cup sour cream

1 teaspoon garlic powder

1 teaspoon onion powder

1 teaspoon sugar

½ teaspoon smoked paprika, plus additional for sprinkling

Kosher salt

Freshly ground black pepper

4 large hard-boiled eggs, cut into large pieces

½ onion, finely diced

½ green bell pepper, finely diced

1 stalk celery, finely diced

Fill a large stockpot with heavily salted water, add the potatoes, and bring to a boil. Cook until tender, 20 to 25 minutes. Drain the potatoes and cut into large chunks when cool enough to handle.

In a large bowl, combine the mayonnaise, relish, mustard, sour cream, garlic powder, onion powder, sugar, paprika, and a pinch of salt and pepper. Add the potato, egg, onion, bell pepper, and celery and toss until combined. Add additional mayo if the salad looks dry. Sprinkle with paprika. Serve immediately or cover and refrigerate until ready to eat.

Shrimp and Grits

Serves 2 to 3

4 slices bacon

1 medium onion, chopped

1 pound medium wild shrimp, peeled and deveined

Sea salt

Freshly ground black pepper

3 tablespoons all-purpose flour, plus more if needed

1 tablespoon garlic powder, plus more if needed

¼ cup canola or vegetable oil, plus more if needed

1 cup hot water

2 tablespoons unsalted butter, if needed

2 cups quick-cooking grits, prepared according to package instructions

½ cup scallions, diagonally sliced

Heat a heavy-bottomed skillet (preferably cast-iron) over medium-high heat. Add the bacon and cook until crispy. Remove and set aside, reserving the drippings. Add the onion to the rendered bacon fat in the skillet and cook on medium-low, stirring, until the onion is slightly tender and the skillet has browned bits, about 3 minutes. Break the bacon into small pieces when it's cool enough to handle.

Meanwhile, put the shrimp in a large bowl. Sprinkle with a few pinches of salt and pepper, the flour, and the garlic powder and toss. Set aside.

Turn the skillet up to medium-high heat and add the canola oil. Test the oil temperature by dropping in a dab of flour. If the flour rises to the top, the oil is hot enough. Add the shrimp, any remaining flour in the bowl, and the bacon and stir with a wooden spoon. Slowly whisk in the hot water and bring to a slight boil, then stir and reduce the heat to a simmer until the gravy thickens and browns, 5 to 10 minutes. If the gravy is too thin, add a slurry to thicken it (see Note). Taste the gravy and add butter and more salt, pepper, or garlic powder if needed.

Serve the shrimp over the prepared grits and top with the scallions.

NOTE: *To make a slurry, mix together 1 tablespoon flour and ⅓ cup hot water in a small bowl.*

Salmon Cakes

Makes 6 or 7 patties

1 14.75-ounce can salmon, drained and soft bones removed

¼ cup yellow onion, finely diced

¼ cup green bell pepper, finely diced

1 large egg

2 tablespoons all-purpose flour

2 teaspoons yellow mustard

2 teaspoons white distilled vinegar

2 teaspoons seafood seasoning, such as Old Bay

Kosher salt

Freshly ground black pepper

Vegetable oil for frying (enough to cover bottom of skillet)

Dill for garnish (optional)

In a large bowl, combine the salmon, onion, bell pepper, egg, flour, mustard, vinegar, seafood seasoning, and a pinch of salt and black pepper. Form the mixture into patties. (I usually get 6 or 7 patties from one can of salmon.)

Heat the oil in a cast-iron skillet or a large, deep frying pan over high heat. When the oil is hot, fry the patties for 3 to 4 minutes on each side, or until golden brown. Garnish with dill and serve warm.

Sea Island Crab Crack with Garlic-Butter Dipping Sauce

Makes 2 dozen crabs

1 6-ounce can seafood seasoning, such as Old Bay, plus more for sprinkling

2 Vidalia onions, coarsely chopped

2 12-ounce cans beer

1 cup (2 sticks) unsalted butter, melted

4 cloves garlic, minced

Pinch of kosher salt

2 dozen live blue crabs

Place a large pot of water over medium-high heat indoors or outside. (I like to use a Lowcountry boil/turkey frying pot.) Add the can of seafood seasoning, onion, and beer and bring to a boil. Boil 10 minutes to allow the flavors to develop.

While the water boils, make the butter sauce. Stir together the butter, garlic, and salt.

Add the crabs to the boiling water. Cook until the crabs are reddish-orange and cooked through, 15 to 20 minutes. Drain the crabs and spread on a table covered with newspaper or butcher paper. Sprinkle with additional seafood seasoning. Serve with the butter dipping sauce.

Johnny Cakes

2 large eggs

1 cup buttermilk, plus more if needed

1 cup yellow cornmeal

1 cup all-purpose flour

2 tablespoons sugar

1 teaspoon baking powder

1 teaspoon kosher salt

¼ cup vegetable oil, plus more for the skillet

Unsalted butter, for the skillet, plus more for serving (optional)

Syrup, for serving (optional)

Preheat the oven to 200°F. Place a wire rack on top of a baking sheet.

In a medium bowl, whisk the eggs and buttermilk until beaten and combined. In a large bowl, whisk together the cornmeal, flour, sugar, baking powder, and salt.

Add the egg mixture to the dry ingredients, stirring until just combined. This is a thick batter, but add a splash of water or buttermilk if the batter feels too thick. Add the vegetable oil and stir until just combined, being careful not to overmix.

In a large cast-iron skillet or griddle over medium heat, melt equal parts butter and vegetable oil (about 2 tablespoons each). Working in batches, use an ice cream scoop to add about 3 tablespoons of the batter to the skillet for each johnny cake. Cook the johnny cakes until bubbles start to appear on the top surface, 2 to 3 minutes. Flip and cook for another 1 to 2 minutes.

Remove the johnny cakes to the wire rack and place in the oven to stay warm. Wipe out the skillet between batches and add more butter and oil before repeating with the remaining batter. Serve with butter and syrup, if using.

The Perfect Pot of Rice

To make the perfect pot of rice, it's very important to rinse the rice before cooking.

This step removes surface starch from the rice grains and yields fluffy rice. So, RINSE, RINSE, RINSE!!!

And here's a helpful rule of thumb: for every cup of rice, use two cups of water.

Serves 4

---

1 cup white long-grain rice

2 cups water

Unsalted butter to your liking

Large pinch of kosher salt

Using a fine-mesh strainer, rinse the rice under cold water until the water runs clear. In a medium saucepan over high heat, bring the 2 cups water to a boil, then add the rice, butter, and salt.

Bring the pan back to a simmer, then lower the heat to medium-high and cook, covered, 18 minutes, or until the rice is tender and the water has been absorbed.

Remove from the heat and let sit, covered, for 5 minutes, then fluff with a fork and serve.

Grandma's Rutabagas

Serves 2 or 3

---

2 1-pound rutabagas, peeled and cut into large chunks

¼ pound smoked meat, on the bone (turkey, ham, or bacon)

2 teaspoons sugar

2 teaspoons garlic powder

2 teaspoons onion powder

Kosher salt to taste, plus more for seasoning

Freshly ground black pepper to taste, plus more for seasoning

Steamed white rice, for serving

Bring a large pot of water to a boil over high heat and add the rutabagas and smoked meat. Stir in the sugar, garlic powder, onion powder, salt, and pepper. Cover, reduce heat to low, and simmer for 90 minutes. The water may boil out if your pot is too hot. If that happens, add 1 cup more. After 90 minutes, taste and season with additional salt and pepper if needed. Serve with steamed white rice.

Deviled Crabs

2 tablespoons unsalted butter

½ large onion, finely chopped

½ stalk celery, finely chopped

½ medium green bell pepper, finely diced

½ medium red bell pepper, finely diced

2 large eggs, lightly beaten

¼ cup Dijon mustard

¼ cup mayonnaise

2 teaspoons dry sherry

2 teaspoons seafood seasoning, such as Old Bay

¼ teaspoon mace

2 pounds fresh blue crabmeat (or 2 8-ounce cans claw meat)

3 cups butter crackers, crushed

Unsalted butter, melted, for topping

Preheat the oven to 375°F.

In a large skillet over medium-high heat, melt the butter, then add the onion, celery, and green and red bell peppers. Cook until slightly softened, 3 to 4 minutes. Remove the pan from the heat and allow the veggies to cool.

In a large bowl, mix the eggs, mustard, mayonnaise, sherry, seafood seasoning, and mace. Add the cooled veggies. Fold in first the crabmeat and then the crushed crackers. Stuff the crab mixture into 10 to 12 cleaned crab shells (equally). Brush a little melted butter on each. Bake for 20 minutes, or until golden brown.

Fried "Fush"

Canola oil, for frying

6 whiting fish fillets

Kosher salt

Freshly ground black pepper

½ cup cornmeal

½ cup all-purpose flour

1 tablespoon Miss Brown's House Seasoning (page 33)

1 lemon

Tartar sauce, for serving

Heat 1½ inches of oil in a deep skillet (I use cast-iron) on medium heat until the oil reaches about 375°F. Line a baking sheet with paper towels and set a wire rack on top.

Clean the fish with cold water and dry just a tad; the fish should be a little wet to help the corn-meal mixture stick to it. Sprinkle a little salt and pepper on the fish. Put the cornmeal, flour, and House Seasoning in a clean paper lunch bag and shake to mix. Add the fish to the flour mixture and shake gently to coat each piece evenly. Transfer the breaded fish to a plate or cut-ting board.

Lay the fish into the oil in batches and fry until they start to float and are golden brown, 3 to 4 minutes. Rest them on the wire rack to let the extra oil run off. Squeeze a little lemon juice on top. Serve with the tartar sauce.

Boiled Peanuts

Grandma planted peanuts with her dad in the nearby fields.
After harvesting, they would boil them and roast them.
Boiled peanuts are a delicacy in the Lowcountry. I served these at my supper club.

Serves 12

---

1 cup kosher salt

1 cup Cajun seasoning

1 lager beer

3 pounds green peanuts or raw peanuts

Combine the salt, Cajun seasoning, and beer in a large stockpot over high heat. Add the peanuts and enough water to cover them. Boil for 2 to 3 hours, or until the peanuts are tender. You can serve the peanuts hot with a little juice from the pot or drain.

Crab Rice

Serves 8 to 12

2 cups chicken stock

1 cup long-grain rice (such as Carolina Gold), rinsed to remove the starch

½ green bell pepper, cut into large pieces

1 stalk celery, cut into large pieces

1 large onion, cut into large pieces

1 clove garlic

2 tablespoons unsalted butter, plus more if needed

1 tablespoon vegetable or canola oil

1 pound crab claw meat, picked for shells

2 generous pinches of Miss Brown's House Seasoning (page 33)

1 large tomato, diced (1 cup)

Fresh parsley roughly chopped, for garnish

Bring the chicken stock to a boil in a medium saucepan. Add the rice. Cover, reduce the heat to low, and simmer until the liquid is absorbed, 15 to 20 minutes. Remove from the heat and fluff with a fork.

While the rice cooks, pulse the bell pepper, celery, onion, and garlic in a food processor until minced. Heat the butter and oil in a large cast-iron skillet over medium-high heat, until the butter melts. Add the minced vegetables. Sauté until the vegetables are tender, about 5 minutes.

Add the crabmeat and House Seasoning. Cook for 5 more minutes, or until the crabmeat has browned. Add additional butter if the vegetables become too dry and begin to brown too quickly. Stir in the cooked rice and tomato. Cover and simmer for 5 additional minutes, until the rice is fluffy. Uncover and sprinkle with parsley before serving.

Nuncey's Fried Chicken

Serves 8

1 whole fryer, feathers removed, cleaned, and cut into 8 pieces

Pinch of kosher salt

Pinch of freshly ground black pepper

Canola or vegetable oil, for frying

2 cups flour

2 teaspoons garlic powder

2 teaspoons onion powder

2 teaspoons paprika

Preheat the oven to 200°F. Set a wire rack on each of 2 rimmed baking sheets.

Make sure the chicken is a little damp, then season it with the salt and pepper. Set the chicken to the side and wash your hands. Pour enough oil into a large Dutch oven or cast-iron skillet to reach about a third of the way up the side; it should be deep enough to submerge the chicken. Heat the oil to 350°F.

Put the flour in a large, clean paper bag. Sprinkle the flour with salt and pepper, and add the garlic powder, onion powder, and paprika. Working with a few pieces at a time, transfer the chicken to the bag with the flour and shake well to coat. Place the coated chicken on the first wire rack.

Fry the chicken in batches until golden brown and the internal temperature measures 165°F, 5 to 6 minutes per side. Remove to the second wire rack and transfer to the oven to stay warm while you cook the rest of the chicken.

Gullah Lima Beans

Serves 8 to 10

2 tablespoons vegetable oil

Smoked turkey neck, bone in, or other smoked meat

1 medium onion, diced

1 pound dried, large lima beans, soaked overnight according to package instructions

2 teaspoons garlic powder

Freshly ground black pepper to taste

Steamed white rice, for serving (optional)

Add oil to a medium to large saucepan on medium-high heat. When the oil is hot, add meat and sauté with the onion for 3 to 4 minutes, until the onion becomes slightly translucent. Add enough water to the pan to submerge the meat. Cover and boil for about 1 hour. Then remove the meat from the pot and drain off about half of the salty water. Put the meat back in the pot and add the lima beans with enough water to cover them, garlic powder, and pepper. Return to a boil, reduce the heat to medium to maintain a slight boil, and cook, covered, for an additional hour. The end result should be slightly soupy. For a hearty meal, serve with white rice.

Sweet Potato Pone

Nonstick cooking spray

4 tablespoons (½ stick) unsalted butter, melted

⅓ cup unpacked light brown sugar

¼ cup molasses

3 large eggs, beaten

½ cup half-and-half

1 teaspoon vanilla extract

½ teaspoon kosher salt

½ teaspoon ground cinnamon

½ teaspoon ground ginger

¼ teaspoon ground nutmeg

1 teaspoon orange zest

3 tablespoons fresh orange juice (from about ½ orange)

2 pounds sweet potatoes (about 3 medium potatoes), peeled and finely grated (about 6 cups grated)

Preheat the oven to 350°F. Lightly spray a 9 × 9-inch baking dish with nonstick cooking spray.

In a large bowl, whisk together the butter, sugar, and molasses. Add the eggs, half-and-half, and vanilla and whisk again until smooth. Add the salt, cinnamon, ginger, nutmeg, orange zest, and orange juice, whisking once more. Fold in the sweet potatoes. Pour the mixture into the prepared baking dish, smooth the top, and cover with foil.

Bake until the center is set and the potatoes are soft, about 40 minutes. Remove the foil and bake until the pone is caramelized on top, another 10 minutes. Cool in the pan to room temperature, about 30 minutes.

NOTE: *For a firmer consistency, place in the refrigerator for at least 2 hours after baking.*

Traditional Cornbread with Molasses Butter

For the cornbread

2 cups yellow self-rising cornmeal

1 cup all-purpose flour

½ teaspoon baking soda

½ teaspoon kosher salt

1 cup (2 sticks) unsalted butter

1 cup whole milk

½ cup buttermilk

2 large eggs

For the molasses butter

8 tablespoons (1 stick) salted butter, at room temperature

2 teaspoons molasses or sorghum syrup

TO MAKE THE CORNBREAD:

Preheat the oven to 425°F.

Combine the cornmeal, flour, baking soda, and salt in a large bowl. Mix well and set aside.

Melt the butter in a large cast-iron skillet or oven-proof sauté pan over medium-high heat. Transfer the melted butter to a medium bowl. Add the whole milk, buttermilk, and eggs, and whisk until blended. Pour the milk mixture into the flour mixture and stir until just combined. Pour the batter back into the skillet and place in the oven.

Bake for 25 minutes, or until a toothpick inserted in the center comes out clean.

TO MAKE THE MOLASSES BUTTER:

Mix the butter and molasses together in a bowl. Serve with the hot cornbread.

Sweet Treats

I loved sweets growing up. And if you ask me, when it comes to authentic southern food, cakes and pies are one of those areas where the rubber meets the road. Our desserts are so unique and region-specific that you cannot fake the funk. A sweet potato pie gone wrong is a mushy mess. And it takes skill to nail a classic pound cake—one that's light and buttery with sweet crusting on the edges.

Believe it or not, I didn't bake much at all until I was grown. Ma wasn't big on making desserts, either. In fact, we loved our southern go-tos so much she'd joke, "Girl, if I baked, we'd be big as a house!" And aside from occasional bread pudding and sweet potato pie, Grandma didn't do desserts much either.

It makes sense when you think about it. Eggs and butter were not easy to come by generations ago. They were relatively expensive, highly perishable, and required a trip to the grocery store. When Grandma was growing up—don't forget, she had thirteen siblings—those were probably luxuries her family could do without.

In my determination to truly train myself in the cooking game, ya girl discovered desserts on her own. Some of my favorites include red velvet cake, peach dump cake, and cheesecake. And I've loved getting the opportunity to be a resident judge on shows like *Spring Baking Championship* and *Gingerbread Showdown*.

Benne Wafers

Makes 24 wafers

8 tablespoons (1 stick) unsalted butter, at room temperature

1 cup packed light brown sugar

1 teaspoon vanilla extract

¼ teaspoon kosher salt

⅛ teaspoon baking soda

1 large egg

1 cup all-purpose flour

1 cup toasted sesame seeds

Nonstick cooking spray, for your hands

Preheat the oven to 350°F. Line 2 baking sheets with parchment paper.

In the bowl of a stand mixer, or in a large bowl with a hand mixer, cream the butter for 30 seconds, until soft. Add the sugar, vanilla, salt, baking soda, and egg and beat until just combined. Add the flour and mix until smooth. Stir in the sesame seeds.

Drop the dough, ½ tablespoon at a time, onto the baking sheets, making sure to leave at least 1 inch between the wafers to allow for spreading. Spray your hands or a spatula with the nonstick spray and press the cookies down to keep them from doming.

Bake until golden brown and starting to crisp on the edges, 10 to 12 minutes. Allow the wafers to cool for 1 minute on the baking sheets, then transfer them to a wire rack to cool completely.

Chewies

Makes 16 squares

4 tablespoons (½ stick) unsalted butter, plus additional softened butter for the baking dish
1 cup packed light brown sugar
1 teaspoon almond extract
1 teaspoon vanilla extract

1 large egg, lightly beaten
¾ cup all-purpose flour
1 teaspoon baking powder
¼ cup chopped pecans
Confectioners' sugar, for dusting

Preheat the oven to 350°F. Butter an 8-inch square baking pan.

Melt the butter in a small saucepan over medium heat. Turn off the heat and let the butter cool slightly, then add the brown sugar, almond extract, and vanilla extract and stir until smooth. Stir in the egg.

In a small bowl, whisk together the flour and baking powder, then fold the flour mixture into the brown sugar mixture. Fold in the pecans. Pour the batter into the prepared baking dish and bake until set around the edges but still loose in the center, about 20 minutes. Let cool completely, then sift confectioners' sugar on top. Cut into 16 squares.

Grandma's Bread Pudding

8 tablespoons (1 stick) unsalted butter, divided

1 apple, cored, peeled, and diced

1 cup purple raisins

2 12-ounce cans evaporated milk

3 large eggs

1 ¾ cups sugar

2 teaspoons cinnamon

2 teaspoons vanilla extract

1 15.25-ounce can fruit cocktail in heavy syrup (do not drain)

2 14-ounce brioche loaves, cut into 1-inch cubes

In a skillet over medium heat, melt 4 tablespoons of the butter, then add the apple and raisins. Cook until the apples are tender and the raisins are rehydrated, 6 to 7 minutes. Add the remaining 4 tablespoons of butter and heat until melted. Turn off the stove and set the skillet to the side.

In a large bowl, whisk together the milk, eggs, and sugar. Add the apple mixture, cinnamon, vanilla, and fruit cocktail then stir to combine. Gently fold the bread cubes into the mixture. Refrigerate for at least 4 hours or overnight.

Preheat the oven to 350°F and coat a 9 × 13-inch baking dish with cooking spray.

Pour the bread mixture into the prepared baking dish. Pack it down using the back of a wooden spoon. Bake until a knife inserted into the middle comes out clean, 45 to 50 minutes.

Sweet Potato Cheesecake

For this recipe, you'll need a 9-inch deep-dish pie plate and a stand mixer or hand mixer.

Serves 6 to 8

For the crust

Nonstick cooking spray

1 ½ cups crushed gingersnap cookies (about 7 ounces or 32 cookies)

⅓ cup packed light brown sugar

6 tablespoons (¾ stick) unsalted butter, melted

Pinch of kosher salt

For the cheesecake filling

8 ounces cream cheese, slightly softened

½ cup sour cream, at room temperature

⅓ cup granulated sugar

¼ teaspoon kosher salt

1 teaspoon vanilla extract

2 large eggs, at room temperature

For the sweet potato topping

½ cup packed light brown sugar

1 teaspoon ground cinnamon

1 teaspoon ground ginger

½ teaspoon freshly ground nutmeg

¼ teaspoon kosher salt

2 cups cooked dark orange sweet potatoes, mashed until very smooth or pureed in a

food processor (about 12 ounces or 2 large sweet potatoes)

¼ cup half-and-half

3 tablespoons unsalted butter, at room temperature

2 teaspoons vanilla extract

2 large eggs, at room temperature

TO MAKE THE CRUST:

Preheat the oven to 350°F. Spray a 9-inch deep-dish pie plate with nonstick cooking spray.

Mix the cookie crumbs, brown sugar, butter, and salt together in a medium bowl until well blended. Press the mixture into the bottom of the pie plate. Bake until the crust is set and feels firm, 7 to 10 minutes. Set aside to cool slightly.

TO MAKE THE CHEESECAKE FILLING:

In the bowl of a stand mixer, or in a large bowl with a hand mixer, combine the cream cheese, sour cream, granulated sugar, and salt, mixing at low speed until the mixture is smooth with no lumps, 3 to 4 minutes. Beat in the vanilla and eggs.

Add the filling to the crust, smooth the top, and chill in the freezer until the filling is sturdy and set up, at least 30 minutes and up to 1 hour.

TO MAKE THE SWEET POTATO TOPPING:

In a medium bowl, whisk together the brown sugar, cinnamon, ginger, nutmeg, and salt. Add the sweet potatoes, half-and-half, butter, vanilla, and eggs and whisk until smooth. Pour slowly over the chilled cheesecake filling.

Place the pie on a baking sheet and bake for 15 minutes. Reduce the oven temperature to 325°F. Cover the edge of the pie with foil if it browns too quickly while baking. Bake until the outside is set and the center still has a slight jiggle, 55 to 60 minutes. Let cool to room temperature before refrigerating until ready to serve.

Miss Brown's Cheesecake Stuffed Strawberry Cake

Serves 12

For the cheesecake center

16 ounces cream cheese, at room temperature

1 cup confectioners' sugar

1 large egg

For the strawberry cake

1 cup (2 sticks) unsalted butter, at room temperature, plus additional for greasing

2 cups granulated sugar

3 large eggs

2 ½ cups all-purpose flour, plus additional for the pan

3 ounces strawberry gelatin

½ teaspoon baking soda

½ teaspoon kosher salt

8 ounces sour cream

1 pint fresh strawberries, diced

For the glaze

2 cups confectioners' sugar

½ teaspoon vanilla extract

2 tablespoons milk, or more if needed

5 to 6 fresh strawberries, sliced, for garnish (optional)

TO MAKE THE CHEESECAKE CENTER:

In a medium bowl with a hand mixer, beat the cream cheese and confectioners' sugar until fluffy and smooth. Add the egg and whisk until combined. Set aside.

TO MAKE THE STRAWBERRY CAKE:

Preheat the oven to 350°F. Grease a tube pan (see Note) with butter and flour the pan thoroughly.

In the bowl of a stand mixer, or in a large bowl with a hand mixer, cream the butter and granulated sugar until pale in color and fluffy. Add the eggs, one at a time, until combined. Scrape the sides and bottom of the bowl.

In a separate bowl, whisk together the flour, gelatin, baking soda, and salt.

With the mixer on low speed, alternate adding the flour mixture and the sour cream to the butter mixture, starting and ending with the flour mixture. Fold in the strawberries. Pour half of the batter into the prepared pan. Using an ice cream scoop, scoop the cheesecake batter evenly on top of the cake batter, making sure to keep the cheesecake batter away from the outer edge of the pan. Pour the remaining batter mixture on top and spread evenly. Bang the pan against the counter to knock out any air bubbles. Place on the center rack of the oven and bake 65 to 70 minutes, or until a wooden skewer inserted in the thickest part of the cake comes out clean.

Allow to cool for at least 15 minutes. Carefully invert the pan onto a cooling rack to cool completely.

TO MAKE THE GLAZE:

In a medium bowl, add the confectioners' sugar and vanilla and slowly whisk in the milk, a little at a time, to make a smooth, slightly thick yet pourable glaze. Cover the cooled cake with the glaze and top with the strawberries, if using.

NOTE: *I use a 16-cup angel food–cake pan for this recipe. You can substitute a 10-cup (or larger) Bundt pan.*

Aunt TC's Lemon-Lime Soda Cake

For the cake

1 ½ cups (3 sticks) unsalted butter, at room temperature, plus additional for greasing

3 cups granulated sugar

5 large eggs

3 cups all-purpose flour, sifted, plus additional for the pan

2 tablespoons lemon extract

1 cup lemon-lime soda, such as 7UP

For the glaze

4 cups sifted confectioners' sugar

⅓ cup milk, plus more if needed

3 tablespoons lemon-lime soda, such as 7Up

2 teaspoons vanilla extract

½ teaspoon lemon extract

TO MAKE THE CAKE:

Preheat the oven to 325°F. Generously grease and flour a fluted 10- to 12-cup Bundt pan.

In a large bowl with an electric mixer, beat the butter and granulated sugar together until creamy and smooth, about 2 minutes. Add the eggs, one at a time, mixing well after each addition. Stir in the flour 1 cup at a time, blending well after each addition, until the batter is smooth. Add the lemon extract and lemon-lime soda and mix. Pour the batter into the prepared pan. Bake until a toothpick inserted in the center of the cake comes out clean, about 75 minutes. Allow the cake to cool completely before adding the glaze.

TO MAKE THE GLAZE:

In a medium bowl with an electric mixer on medium speed, beat the confectioners' sugar, milk, lemon-lime soda, vanilla extract, and lemon extract together until the glaze is smooth and thick yet pourable.

Pierce holes in the cake with a skewer. Pour ¼ cup glaze over the cake. Flip the cake onto a serving plate, remove the pan, and pour the remaining glaze on top. The cake can be served immediately, but it tastes even better the longer it sits.

My Favorite Red Velvet Cake

For the cake

Nonstick cooking spray

2 ¾ cups cake flour

¼ cup unsweetened cocoa powder, plus more for dusting pans

1 teaspoon baking soda

½ teaspoon kosher salt

1 cup buttermilk, at room temperature

2 tablespoons red food coloring

1 tablespoon vanilla extract

2 teaspoons white vinegar

2 cups granulated sugar

1 cup vegetable oil

8 tablespoons (1 stick) unsalted butter, softened

3 large eggs, at room temperature

For the frosting

1 cup (2 sticks) unsalted butter, softened

½ teaspoon kosher salt

12 ounces cream cheese, softened

3 ½ cups confectioners' sugar, plus more if needed

2 teaspoons vanilla extract

2 tablespoons heavy cream, as needed

½ cup finely chopped pecans, for garnish (optional)

TO MAKE THE CAKE:

Preheat the oven to 350°F. Spray two 9-inch cake pans well with nonstick cooking spray, dust with cocoa powder, line the bottoms of the pans with parchment paper, and set aside.

In a medium bowl, whisk together the flour, cocoa powder, baking soda, and salt and set aside. In a small bowl, stir together the buttermilk, food coloring, vanilla, and vinegar and set aside.

In the bowl of a stand mixer fitted with a paddle attachment, or in a large bowl with a hand mixer, beat the granulated sugar, oil, and butter on high speed until light and fluffy, about 2 minutes. Add the eggs, one at time, beating well after each addition. Scrape the bottom of the bowl with a rubber spatula and briefly beat again to ensure everything is combined.

Alternately add the flour mixture and the buttermilk mixture in three parts and mix on medium speed just until everything is combined. Divide the batter evenly between the two prepared pans, using a large offset spatula or knife to smooth the top. Bake until a toothpick inserted in the middle of the cakes comes out clean, 28 to 30 minutes. Cool completely in the pan, 20 to 30 minutes.

TO MAKE THE FROSTING:

In the bowl of a stand mixer fitted with a paddle attachment, or in a large bowl with a hand mixer, beat the butter and salt on high speed for 1 minute. Add the cream cheese and beat until combined and fluffy, about 1 minute. With the mixer on medium speed, beat in the confectioners' sugar in three additions until combined. Beat in the vanilla until combined. If the frosting is too stiff, beat in the heavy cream, as needed.

When the cake is completely cool, level the top of each layer with a bread knife. Place one layer on a cake turntable or plate and spread about a third of the frosting evenly on top, using a large offset spatula or knife. Place the second layer on top and use the remaining frosting to cover the top and sides of the cake. Sprinkle with the pecans, if using.

Vanilla Bean Buttermilk Pie

For the crust

1 ¼ cups all-purpose flour, plus more for dusting

2 teaspoons sugar

½ teaspoon kosher salt

8 tablespoons (1 stick) cold unsalted butter, cubed

⅓ cup ice-cold water

For the filling

1 ½ cups sugar

1 ¼ cups buttermilk, at room temperature

4 large eggs, plus 1 yolk, at room temperature

8 tablespoons (1 stick) unsalted butter, melted

Seeds from 1 vanilla bean (see Note)

1 teaspoon vanilla extract

½ teaspoon kosher salt

¼ cup all-purpose flour

Whipped cream, for serving

TO MAKE THE CRUST:

Put the flour, sugar and salt in a food processor and pulse to combine. Add the butter and pulse until the butter forms pea-size pieces. Add the water and continue to pulse until the dough begins to come together. Press the dough into a disc and wrap in plastic wrap. Refrigerate until thoroughly chilled, at least 1 hour. After 1 hour, preheat the oven to 350°F. On a lightly floured surface, roll the dough into a disk about 11 to 12 inches wide. Line the bottom of a 9-inch pie plate with the dough, then crimp the edges. Refrigerate while you make the filling.

TO MAKE THE FILLING:

Whisk together the sugar, buttermilk, eggs, egg yolk, melted butter, vanilla seeds, vanilla extract, and salt until well blended. Sprinkle the flour on top and whisk just until incorporated.

Remove the pie plate from the fridge. Place the pie plate on a baking sheet, then pour the filling over the dough. Bake on the bottom rack until the top of the pie is golden brown and set around the edges and the center has a slight jiggle, about 1 hour. If the crust begins to get too brown, but the filling isn't ready, cover the edges loosely with foil. Let the pie cool to room temperature before slicing. Serve with whipped cream.

NOTE: *To scrape the seeds from a vanilla bean, place the bean on a cutting surface. Cut the bean lengthwise using the tip of a paring knife. Then scrape the seeds from the inside of the pod using the point or the edge of the knife.*

Nana's Puddin'

For the pudding

3 cups whole milk

1 cup sugar

⅔ cup all-purpose flour

¼ teaspoon kosher salt

6 large egg yolks

2 teaspoons vanilla extract

14 ounces sweetened condensed milk

1 12-ounce container extra-creamy frozen whipped topping

For the assembly

1 11-ounce box vanilla wafers, plus more, crushed, for garnish (optional)

5 medium-size ripe bananas, sliced, plus more for garnish (optional)

1 12-ounce container extra-creamy frozen whipped topping, for garnish (optional)

TO MAKE THE PUDDING:

In a large saucepan over medium-low heat, combine the milk, sugar, flour, and salt. Cook, stirring constantly, until the mixture becomes thick, about 8 minutes. In a small bowl, beat the egg yolks lightly. Whisk a little bit of the milk mixture into the egg yolks until tempered. Slowly add the egg yolks to the milk mixture, and whisk until combined. Cook 2 more minutes to cook the eggs, stirring constantly. Remove the pan from the heat, add the vanilla, and fold in the sweetened condensed milk. Let stand until cooled, about 30 minutes (see Note). Once cooled, fold in the whipped topping.

TO ASSEMBLE:

Arrange a single layer of vanilla wafers in the bottom of a 13 × 9-inch baking dish. Add a layer of sliced bananas on top. Cover with half of the pudding. Repeat the layers. Garnish with the additional whipped topping, crushed vanilla wafers, and bananas, if using. Cover and chill until ready to serve.

NOTE: *If you're short on time, you can chill the custard over an ice bath for 10 minutes instead of letting it stand.*

Blackberry Cobbler

1 ½ cups granulated sugar, divided

1 cup all-purpose flour

1 tablespoon baking powder

½ teaspoon kosher salt

1 cup half-and-half

8 tablespoons (1 stick) unsalted butter, melted

6 cups blackberries frozen or fresh

½ cup packed light brown sugar

2 tablespoons water

1 tablespoon freshly squeezed lemon juice

1 teaspoon ground cinnamon

1 teaspoon ground nutmeg

Ice cream, for serving (optional)

Preheat the oven to 375°F.

In a large bowl, whisk together 1 cup of the granulated sugar, the flour, baking powder, and salt. Stir in the half-and-half, mixing just until combined.

Add the butter to a 9 × 13-inch baking dish, tilting to coat evenly. Pour the batter over the butter in the baking dish, then set aside.

In a small saucepan over medium-high heat, bring the berries, brown sugar, water, lemon juice, cinnamon, nutmeg, and the remaining ½ cup granulated sugar to a boil. Cook for 2 minutes more. Spoon the berry mixture over the batter in the baking dish without disturbing the batter.

Bake until golden brown and puffed on top, 45 to 50 minutes. Let cool slightly before serving with a scoop of ice cream or enjoy it without.

Hummingbird Sheet Cake

For the cake

Nonstick cooking spray

3 cups all-purpose flour, plus more for the pan

1 ½ teaspoons ground cinnamon

1 teaspoon baking soda

1 teaspoon kosher salt

½ teaspoon ground nutmeg

2 cups granulated sugar

1 ½ cups canola oil

1 cup sweetened coconut flakes

2 teaspoons vanilla extract

3 large eggs

3 very ripe large bananas, mashed (1 ½ to 2 cups)

1 8-ounce can crushed pineapple

1 cup pecans, toasted and chopped

For the frosting

8 tablespoons (1 stick) unsalted butter, softened

¼ teaspoon kosher salt

8 ounces cream cheese, softened

3 ½ cups confectioners' sugar

1 teaspoon vanilla extract

1 to 2 tablespoons heavy cream, as needed

Dried pineapple rings, for garnish (optional)

¼ cup finely chopped pecans, for garnish (optional)

TO MAKE THE CAKE:

Preheat the oven to 350°F. Spray a 9 × 13-inch metal pan with nonstick cooking spray and dust the inside lightly with flour, knocking the excess out.

In a large bowl, whisk together the flour, cinnamon, baking soda, salt, and nutmeg.

In a separate medium bowl, beat together the granulated sugar, oil, coconut, vanilla, eggs, banana, and pineapple. Pour the wet ingredients into the dry ingredients and whisk until completely combined. Fold in the pecans. Pour the batter in the prepared pan. Bake until a toothpick inserted in the center comes out clean or the cake bounces back when lightly pressed with a finger, 30 to 35 minutes. Allow to cool for 30 minutes. Transfer from the pan to a wire rack and cool completely. Once completely cooled, level the top using a serrated knife.

TO MAKE THE FROSTING:

Meanwhile, in the bowl of a stand mixer fitted with a paddle attachment, or in a large bowl with a hand mixer, beat the butter and salt on high speed for 1 minute. Add the cream cheese and beat until combined and fluffy, about 1 minute. With the mixer on medium speed, beat in the confectioners' sugar in three batches until combined. Beat in the vanilla until combined. If the frosting is too stiff, beat in the heavy cream, as needed.

Spread the frosting over the cake and decorate with the pineapple rings and pecans, if using. Cut into 12 equal pieces and serve.

Edisto Lemon Pie

For the crust

1 ½ cups pretzel crumbs (from about 4 cups of salted pretzels)

⅓ cup packed light brown sugar

6 tablespoons (¾ stick) unsalted butter, melted

For the filling and topping

2 14-ounce cans sweetened condensed milk

Juice of 4 freshly squeezed lemons

Zest of 1 lemon

4 large egg yolks

1 jar lemon curd

Whipped cream, for garnish (optional)

Lemon slices, for garnish (optional)

Lemon-peel curls, for garnish (optional)

Preheat the oven to 350°F.

TO MAKE THE CRUST:
In a food processor, pulse the pretzel crumbs and brown sugar. Pour the melted butter into the chute of the food processor. Pulse again until the ingredients are well combined. Press the crust onto the bottom and sides of a pie plate and set aside.

TO MAKE THE FILLING AND TOPPING:
In a bowl, whisk the sweetened condensed milk, lemon juice, lemon zest, and egg yolks to combine, then pour the mixture into the prepared crust. Drop dollops of lemon curd on top, and use a toothpick to swirl the curd into the filling mixture until it has a marbled look. Bake until the pie is firm around the edges but slightly jiggly in the center, about 20 minutes. Cool completely before serving. I suggest letting it set up overnight. Garnish with whipped cream, lemon slices, and lemon-peel curls, if using.

Mrs. Drayton's Inspired Ice Box Cake

Serves 12

2 3.5-ounce packages coconut cream pudding mix

⅓ cup confectioners' sugar

3 cups heavy cream

2 8-ounce containers frozen whipped topping, thawed, divided

1 20-ounce can crushed pineapple, with its juice

1 14.4-ounce box graham crackers (I like honey-flavored)

1 cup chopped pecans, for garnish

Maraschino cherries, for garnish

In the bowl of a stand mixer, or in a large bowl with a hand mixer, mix the pudding, confectioners' sugar, cream, 8 ounces whipped topping, and the pineapple and its juice.

Place a single layer of graham crackers in a 9 × 13-inch casserole dish, and top with half of the pudding mixture. Add another layer of graham crackers and the remaining pudding mixture. Top with a final layer of graham crackers and the remaining 8 ounces of whipped topping. Refrigerate for 4 to 6 hours or overnight. Garnish with the cherries and pecans before serving.

Butter Pecan Pie Cheesecake
with Browned Butter Sauce

Serves 12

For the crust

Nonstick cooking spray

2 cups graham cracker crumbs

½ cup finely chopped pecans

⅓ cup packed light brown sugar

¼ teaspoon kosher salt

6 tablespoons (¾ stick) salted butter, melted

For the filling

1 cup granulated sugar

½ cup packed light brown sugar

2 tablespoons cornstarch

32 ounces cream cheese, at room temperature

1 cup sour cream, at room temperature

5 large eggs, at room temperature

1 teaspoon vanilla extract

For the sauce

6 tablespoons (¾ stick) unsalted butter

1 cup packed light brown sugar

⅓ cup whole milk

1 ½ cups pecan halves

TO MAKE THE CRUST:

Preheat the oven to 350°F. Lightly spray a 9-inch springform pan with nonstick cooking spray and place on a baking sheet.

In a food processor, pulse the graham crackers and pecans until fine, then add the brown sugar and salt and pulse until well combined. Drizzle in the melted butter and stir until the mixture resembles damp sand. Press the crumbs into an even layer on the bottom of the prepared pan. Bake the crust until firm, about 10 minutes, then let cool.

TO MAKE THE FILLING:

In a small bowl, stir together the granulated sugar, brown sugar, and cornstarch. In the bowl of a stand mixer, or in a large bowl with a hand mixer, beat the cream cheese and sour cream until smooth and fluffy. Add the sugar mixture, ½ cup at a time, beating until smooth. Add the eggs, one at a time, and beat until well combined, scraping down the sides of the bowl. Add the vanilla and continue to mix, making sure everything is incorporated.

(cont.)

Pour the filling over the top of the graham cracker crust. Knock out any air bubbles by gently tapping the pan on the counter. Double-wrap the bottom of the pan with foil, sealing it tightly to prevent water from getting into the pan. Place the springform pan into a larger pan and pour very hot water into the outer pan until it is about ¾ inch deep, making sure the water level doesn't come up higher than the foil.

Bake until the edges of the cheesecake are set and the center still jiggles, 60 to 70 minutes. Crack the oven door and allow the cake to cool in the oven for 1 to 2 hours.

Remove the cake from the oven and refrigerate for at least 4 hours and preferably overnight. After the cheesecake is fully set, remove it from the pan.

TO MAKE THE SAUCE:
In a small saucepan over medium high heat, melt the butter, stirring occasionally. When the butter starts to foam and turns amber with brown bits, lower the heat to low and add the brown sugar. Melt the sugar in the butter, then slowly whisk in the milk. Turn the heat back up to medium-high and bring the sauce to a slight boil. Once the ingredients have been fully incorporated, stir and set to the side to cool. The sauce will thicken up once cooled.

In a medium skillet over medium high heat, quickly toast the pecans until they begin to darken and become fragrant. Do not leave the pecans unattended; they will burn fairly quickly. Remove from heat.

Spread the pecans on top of the cheesecake and pour the browned butter sauce over the pecans. Slice and enjoy.

Berry Cream Cheese Hand Pies

For this recipe, you'll need a 5-inch round cookie cutter.

Makes 8 hand pies

2 cups fresh or frozen blackberries

⅔ cup granulated sugar

1 tablespoon cornstarch

Juice of 1 lemon

Zest of 1 lemon

1 box premade pie crusts (2 rounds)

All-purpose flour, for dusting

2 ounces cream cheese, cut into 8 cubes and chilled

1 large egg, lightly beaten

1 tablespoon water

¼ cup raw or turbinado sugar

Preheat the oven to 375°F. Line 2 baking sheets with parchment paper.

In a medium saucepan over medium heat, cook the blackberries and granulated sugar, mashing the berries with a potato masher or the back of a spoon until they start to break down and release their juices, about 2 minutes. Mix the cornstarch and lemon juice in a small bowl. Add the cornstarch mixture and the lemon zest to the berries and stir until there are no more lumps. Continue to stir until the filling begins to thicken, 2 to 3 minutes. Remove from the heat, transfer to a bowl, and let cool slightly.

Roll one of the pie crusts out on a lightly floured surface until about ⅛-inch thick. Use a 5-inch round cookie cutter, or the rim of a 5-inch bowl, to cut out as many rounds as you can. Repeat with the remaining pie crust, gather the scraps, and reroll as necessary to get 8 rounds.

Place 1 cube of cream cheese and 1 tablespoon of filling in the center of a round. Fold the dough over into a crescent and crimp the edge with a fork. Place on one of the prepared baking sheets. Repeat with the remaining pie crust rounds, cream cheese, and filling.

Whisk together the egg and water in a small bowl. Brush the filled hand pies with the egg wash, sprinkle with the raw sugar, and cut small vents into the tops. (If you brush the hand pies after venting, the egg will cover the vents!) Bake until the pies are golden brown, 20 to 25 minutes, and serve fresh out of the oven.

Bryon's Peach Dump Cake

Nonstick cooking spray

8 tablespoons (1 stick) unsalted butter, very cold, sliced evenly into tablespoons

1 21-ounce box Krusteaz Cinnamon Swirl Crumb Cake & Muffin Mix

2 pounds frozen peach slices

¼ cup packed light brown sugar

½ cup granulated sugar

2 tablespoons cornstarch

1 tablespoon freshly squeezed lemon juice

1 teaspoon vanilla extract

Vanilla ice cream, for serving

Preheat the oven to 350°F. Spray a 9-inch square baking dish or a 10-inch cast-iron skillet with nonstick cooking spray. In a food processor, combine the butter and cake mix, reserving the cinnamon sugar packet for later. Pulse until the butter turns into little pea-size granules. Set aside.

In a medium bowl, combine the peaches, brown sugar, granulated sugar, cornstarch, lemon juice, and vanilla. Toss to coat the peaches. Pour the mixture into the prepared baking dish, then spread the cake mix over the top in an even layer. Sprinkle with the cinnamon sugar from the box. Cover the baking dish with aluminum foil and bake until the top is puffed and golden and the fruit is bubbling, about 40 minutes. Turn the oven up to 400°F, remove the foil, and continue baking for 5 minutes more.

Let the cake cool slightly before scooping and serving with vanilla ice cream.

Salted Georgia Peanut Pie

For the pie

1 9-inch deep-dish frozen pie shell, thawed

1 ½ cups honey-roasted peanuts

1 cup packed light brown sugar

3 large eggs, lightly beaten

⅓ cup molasses

¼ cup chunky peanut butter

4 tablespoons (½ stick) salted or unsalted butter, melted

1 teaspoon vanilla

¼ teaspoon kosher salt or flaked sea salt

For the whipped cream

1 cup heavy whipping cream

¼ cup confectioners' sugar

Seeds from ½ vanilla bean

TO MAKE THE PIE:

Preheat the oven to 350°F.

Place the pie shell on a baking sheet. Spread the peanuts in the bottom of the shell. In a large bowl, combine the brown sugar, eggs, molasses, peanut butter, butter, vanilla, and salt. Whisk until completely combined. Pour the filling gently into the pie shell on top of the nuts. Bake until the filling is set and the pie is puffed and golden brown, 45 to 50 minutes. Start checking the crust after about 30 minutes, and cover with foil if the crust starts to become too dark. Remove from the oven and transfer to a wire rack. Let cool completely, about 2 hours.

TO MAKE THE WHIPPED CREAM:

While the pie is cooling, in a medium bowl beat the cream, confectioners' sugar, and vanilla seeds to soft peaks. Refrigerate until ready to serve with slices of cooled pie.

Oreo Brownie Delight

Makes 16 squares

For the brownie layer

Nonstick cooking spray

½ cup unsweetened cocoa powder, plus extra for the pan

1 cup all-purpose flour

¼ teaspoon kosher salt

1 ½ cups sugar

12 tablespoons (1 ½ sticks) unsalted butter, melted

2 large eggs

1 tablespoon canola oil

1 teaspoon vanilla extract

¾ cup mini chocolate chips

About 16 Oreo cookies

For the cheesecake layer

24 ounces cream cheese, at room temperature

¾ cup sugar

2 large eggs

2 teaspoons vanilla

12 Oreo cookies, roughly chopped

Chocolate sauce, for serving (optional)

Preheat the oven to 325°F. Spray a 9 × 13-inch baking dish with nonstick cooking spray. I like to add a little dusting of cocoa powder as well. Set aside.

TO MAKE THE BROWNIE LAYER:

In a medium bowl, combine the cocoa powder, flour, and salt. Set aside. In a large bowl, mix together the sugar, butter, eggs, oil, and vanilla. Add the flour mixture to the butter mixture and stir to combine. Fold in chocolate chips. Pour the batter into the prepared baking dish. Place the Oreo cookies on top of the batter. Space them out evenly.

TO MAKE THE CHEESECAKE LAYER:

In a large bowl, beat together the cream cheese and sugar until the mixture becomes fluffy. Add the eggs, one at a time, beating slowly, then add the vanilla, stirring until combined. Pour the cheesecake batter on top of the brownie layer, spreading it evenly. Sprinkle the chopped Oreos on top. Bake until the edges are almost golden brown and the center is a little jiggly, about 45 minutes. Cool, then refrigerate for at least 2 hours or overnight. Serve with a drizzle of chocolate sauce, if using.

Toasted Coconut Cake

For the cake

8 tablespoons (1 stick) unsalted butter, at room temperature, plus more for greasing the pan

2 ¾ cups cake flour, plus more for flouring the pan

4 large eggs, at room temperature

1 teaspoon baking powder

½ teaspoon baking soda

½ teaspoon kosher salt

1 ⅔ cups granulated sugar

½ cup coconut oil

1 cup sweetened cream of coconut

1 tablespoon vanilla extract

1 cup buttermilk

For the coconut cream cheese frosting

12 ounces cream cheese, at room temperature

10 tablespoons (1 ¼ sticks) unsalted butter, at room temperature

½ teaspoon coconut extract

Pinch of kosher salt

5 cups confectioners' sugar, plus more if needed

1 tablespoon milk, if needed

2 cups sweetened coconut flakes, toasted

TO MAKE THE CAKE:

Preheat the oven to 350°F. Butter two 8-inch cake pans, then fit each with a parchment paper round. Butter and flour the parchment.

Separate the eggs into whites and yolks. Set the yolks aside. Beat the egg whites to stiff peaks, then set aside until ready to use.

In a medium bowl, whisk together the flour, baking powder, baking soda, and salt. In the bowl of a stand mixer, or in a large bowl with a hand mixer, beat together the granulated sugar, butter, and coconut oil until light and fluffy, about 2 minutes. Add the egg yolks, coconut cream, and vanilla and beat until just combined. Alternately add the buttermilk and flour mixture to the butter mixture, being careful not to overmix. Gently fold in the beaten egg whites until completely incorporated, but keep the volume!

Divide the batter evenly between the prepared cake pans.

Bake until a toothpick inserted in the middle of the cakes comes out clean, 25 to 30 minutes.

Let the cakes cool for about 5 minutes, then invert them onto a cooling rack to cool completely.

TO MAKE THE COCONUT CREAM CHEESE FROSTING:

Meanwhile, in the bowl of a stand mixer or in a large bowl with a hand mixer, beat the cream cheese and butter until very smooth, about 2 minutes. Add the coconut extract and salt, then slowly add the confectioners' sugar, beating it in a little at a time. Beat until all the sugar is combined and the frosting is stiff but still light and fluffy. Add more sugar if it is too loose, or the milk if it is too thick. Set aside at room temperature until you are ready to decorate.

If the cakes have domed at all, shave down any uneven parts to make the tops of the cakes flat and smooth.

Spread 1 tablespoon frosting on a cake plate or stand; this will help keep the cake in place while you decorate. Place one layer cut-side up on the plate. Dollop about 1 cup of frosting on top of the cake and spread it in an even layer using a spatula, knife, or spoon. Place the second layer cut-side up on top of the first. Dollop 2 cups of frosting on top of the cake and smooth it over the top and down the sides. Repeat with any remaining frosting until the outside of the cake is frosted and smooth. Using your hands, press the toasted coconut into the sides of the cake and sprinkle it on the top, so that the entire cake is covered in toasted coconut.

Refrigerate until ready to serve. Serve at room temperature or chilled.

Breakin' the Fast

Okay now, y'all—what we are *not* about to do is forget about breakfast! C'mon now, you know it's the most important meal of the day. When Grandma was coming up, it was usually the men who went out to work. And their laboring days were long and hard. Back then, the women woke up before dawn to make sure their husbands were good and ready for the manual labor in front of them. Trust and believe, quick food was not gonna cut it. They needed a hearty meal. And the women fixed meat and eggs and grits and potatoes.

It's probably because of that tradition that Ma always made breakfast—even if she was working the night shift. I mean, I don't care what was going on, I was not getting out of the house without breaking the fast. I'm going to show you how to make some good food—fast, if need be. And you won't hear me say "microwave." *What?* I don't know her!

Seriously, though, I get it. A midweek morning is maybe not going to be the day you sit your family and friends down for homemade Country Garlic Gravy and Biscuits (page 124). We're all busy. Just because you're short on time, though, it doesn't mean you can't eat something fresh and delicious to power you through your day. Many a morning, especially weekdays, Ma and I were rushing. She had to take me to school and get to work on time. On those days, that all-important meal was eaten in the car— all kinds of the most delicious breakfast sandwiches you can imagine—sometimes eggs, sausage, or the best BLT you've ever tasted. Try as I might, I never did manage to convince Ma to make a couple dozen sandwiches for me to take to school. I could've made a small fortune off of her breakfasts. I just know it.

I sure did love those sandwiches. But on the weekends? Baby! That's when breakfast took center stage. More time meant lots more food. Shout out to Grandma's Savory Bread Pudding (page 128). And can I get a witness for some Black Cherry Muffins (page 148)? I must admit, with my busy schedule, breaking the fast for me might mean a delicious smoothie—homemade, of course. But I still enjoy breakfast to this day!

Fluffy Buttermilk Biscuits

Serves 4 to 6	
2 cups all-purpose flour, plus extra for dusting	8 tablespoons (1 stick) unsalted butter, very cold, cubed
1 tablespoon baking powder	¾ cup buttermilk, plus more as needed
¼ teaspoon baking soda	4 tablespoons (½ stick) unsalted butter, melted, divided
1 teaspoon kosher salt	

Preheat the oven to 450°F. Place a 10 1/2-inch cast-iron skillet in the oven to heat.

In a large bowl, combine the flour, baking powder, baking soda, and salt. Mix very well. Use your hands or a pastry cutter to work the cold butter into the flour until the butter forms crumbs the size of large peas. Slowly pour in the buttermilk, then mix with your hands until the mixture starts to form a dough. Add more buttermilk if it feels too dry. As soon as the dough comes together, transfer to a floured work surface. Press the dough into a square and fold it over itself to create layers, using additional flour to keep the dough from sticking. Shape into a ½-inch-thick rectangle. Use a 2- to 3-inch biscuit cutter to cut out biscuits, rerolling the scraps to use all the dough.

Take the skillet out of the oven and add 2 tablespoons of the melted butter. Place the biscuits in the skillet, touching, then lightly brush the tops with the remaining 2 tablespoons butter then brush with a little buttermilk.

Bake until lightly golden brown, 13 to 14 minutes. Let cool for a few minutes, then serve.

Country Garlic Gravy and Biscuits

4 tablespoons (½ stick) unsalted butter, divided

½ yellow onion, finely diced

1 16-ounce country pork or turkey sausage roll, such as Jimmy Dean Sausage Roll

2 cloves garlic, minced (or 2 teaspoons garlic powder)

¼ cup all-purpose flour

2 cups whole milk, at room temperature

Kosher salt to taste

2 teaspoons freshly ground black pepper

4 to 6 Fluffy Buttermilk Biscuits (page 123)

Scallions, diced, for garnish (optional)

In a large skillet over medium-high heat, melt 2 tablespoons of the butter, then add the onion, cooking for 2 to 3 minutes. Add the sausage and garlic and cook until the sausage turns completely brown. Stir in the flour and the remaining 2 tablespoons of butter, then slowly add the milk. Cook until the gravy begins to thicken. Add a heavy pinch of salt and the black pepper, seasoning to taste. Ladle the gravy over the biscuits and top with the scallions, if using, for a pop of color.

Fried Grits Balls with Tasso Ham

Canola oil, for frying

½ cup diced tasso or country ham

2 ½ cups cooked grits

½ cup grated creamy smoked gouda cheese

½ cup shredded sharp or extra sharp white cheddar cheese

½ cup all-purpose flour

2 teaspoons Miss Brown's House Seasoning (page 33), divided

3 large eggs

1 cup panko breadcrumbs

Kosher salt

Hot Peppa Jelly (page 164; optional)

Fill a large Dutch oven two-thirds full with oil and heat over medium-high heat to 360°F.

In a large heavy-bottomed skillet over medium-high heat, put 2 tablespoons oil. Add the ham and cook just until browned, 4 to 5 minutes. Remove with a slotted spoon to a large bowl. Add the grits, gouda cheese, and cheddar cheese to the ham and stir until combined. Using wet hands, scoop out ¼ cup of the grits mixture, roll it into a ball, and place it on a platter or large plate. Repeat until all the grits mixture is used.

In a shallow bowl, whisk together the flour and 1 teaspoon of the House Seasoning. In another shallow bowl, lightly beat the eggs. In a third shallow bowl, combine the breadcrumbs and the remaining 1 teaspoon of the House Seasoning. Dip each grits ball into the flour mixture and shake to remove any excess before dipping it into the egg and then into the breadcrumbs, spinning it to coat completely.

Add the grits balls to the Dutch oven in batches, frying until brown on all sides, about 5 minutes. Remove to a sheet pan topped with a wire rack and immediately sprinkle with salt. As an option, serve with Hot Peppa Jelly.

Savory Bread Pudding

Serves 8

Nonstick cooking spray

1 14-ounce loaf of bread (white bread, French bread, buns, or whatever you have on hand)

6 tablespoons (¾ stick) unsalted butter, melted, divided

1 medium yellow onion, chopped

1 16-ounce country pork or turkey sausage roll, such as Jimmy Dean Sausage Roll

6 large eggs

2 cups half-and-half

2 teaspoons garlic powder

1 teaspoon rubbed sage

1 teaspoon dried parsley

Kosher salt to taste

Freshly ground black pepper

2 cups shredded white cheddar cheese

½ cup shredded Havarti cheese (or your favorite white melting cheese)

2 scallions, diced

Preheat the oven to 375°F and spray a 9 × 13-inch baking dish with nonstick cooking spray.

Cut the bread into 1-inch cubes, place them in a large bowl, and set aside. In a large skillet over medium-high heat, add 3 tablespoons of the melted butter, and sauté the onion for 2 to 3 minutes. Add the sausage and cook until brown, then transfer the sausage mixture to the bowl with the bread.

In a separate bowl, whisk together the eggs, half-and-half, garlic powder, sage, parsley, and a pinch of salt and pepper. Pour this custard over the bread and sausage. Add the cheddar and Havarti cheeses, the remaining 3 tablespoons of melted butter, and the scallions and toss until the bread is thoroughly soaked. Pour the mixture evenly into the prepared baking dish. I like to pat the top down with a spatula to smooth it. Bake uncovered until golden brown, about 45 minutes.

Waterfront Omelet with Creamy Sherry Butter Sauce

For the sauce

4 tablespoons (½ stick) unsalted butter

1 tablespoon finely chopped shallot or red onion

1 small clove garlic, minced

2 tablespoons all-purpose flour

1 cup heavy whipping cream

3 tablespoons sherry (or a very dry white wine of your choice)

⅓ cup grated Parmesan cheese

Seafood seasoning, such as Old Bay

Freshly ground black pepper

For the omelet

1 tablespoon olive oil, divided

½ medium onion, diced

½ pound shrimp, cleaned and deveined

Miss Brown's House Seasoning (page 33)

½ pound lump crabmeat (or claw meat), picked for shells

1 large beefsteak tomato, seeds and core discarded, diced, plus more for garnish (optional)

6 large eggs

2 tablespoons milk

4 tablespoons (½ stick) unsalted butter, divided

Chopped fresh parsley leaves, for garnish (optional)

TO MAKE THE SAUCE:

In a small saucepan over medium-low heat, add the butter, shallot, and garlic. Sauté for about 1 minute. Add the flour and stir. Whisk in the heavy cream, then the sherry; bring to a simmer. The sauce should start to thicken slightly. Reduce the heat to low simmer for 5 minutes. Add the Parmesan, seafood seasoning, and a pinch of pepper. Taste and adjust to your liking. Keep on low heat and stir occasionally until ready to serve.

TO MAKE THE OMELET:

Heat a little of the oil in a large nonstick skillet over medium high heat. When hot, add the onion and shrimp and sprinkle with a pinch of the House Seasoning. Once the shrimp turns slightly opaque, add the crabmeat and tomato, gently toss, then turn off the heat. Now grab a bowl and whisk together the eggs and milk and set aside. Transfer the seafood mixture from the skillet to a separate bowl. Clean the skillet and return it to the stove. Heat to medium and add little oil and 2 tablespoons of the butter to the skillet (the bottom of the skillet should be well greased). Add about 1 cup of the egg and milk mixture to the skillet, loosen up the sides with a spatula, and cook until the omelet is lightly browned underneath and the top is almost set. Spoon the seafood mixture over half of the omelet, add some of the sherry cream sauce, then fold the omelet in half. Turn the heat off and cook for 2 more minutes. Serve with additional sherry sauce on top. Garnish with the parsley and additional chopped tomatoes, if using.

Fried Chicken and Pancakes with Spicy Syrup

Makes 8 pancakes

For the syrup
1 cup maple syrup (use your favorite)
2 tablespoons salted or unsalted butter

1 tablespoon hot sauce
Pinch of cayenne pepper

For the chicken
4 8-ounce boneless, skinless chicken breasts, cut lengthwise into 1-inch-wide strips
2 cups buttermilk
3 tablespoons Miss Brown's House Seasoning (page 33), divided

2 cups all-purpose flour
1 teaspoon freshly ground black pepper
1 teaspoon baking powder
1 teaspoon kosher salt
1 teaspoon confectioners' sugar
Vegetable or canola oil, for frying

For the pancakes
1 ½ cups all-purpose flour
2 tablespoons sugar
2 teaspoons baking powder
½ teaspoon baking soda
½ teaspoon kosher salt
¾ cup ricotta cheese

½ cup milk
1 teaspoon vanilla extract
2 large eggs
Vegetable oil, for cooking
2 tablespoons butter, for cooking

TO MAKE THE SYRUP:
In a small saucepan over medium heat, whisk the syrup, butter, hot sauce, and cayenne pepper. Once the ingredients are combined, let the pot sit on low until ready to serve. (I like my syrup warm.)

TO MAKE THE CHICKEN:
Put the chicken in a large bowl, and add the buttermilk and 1 tablespoon of the House Seasoning. Let the chicken marinate in the refrigerator for at least 4 hours. (You can do this step the night before cooking.)

Combine the flour, the remaining 2 tablespoons of House Seasoning, the pepper, baking powder, salt, and confectioners' sugar in a large, shallow dish or clean paper lunch bag.

Remove the chicken from the buttermilk and dredge each piece in the seasoned flour. Shake off any excess and transfer to a plate.

Fill a large cast-iron skillet halfway with oil and fit the skillet with a deep-frying thermometer. Heat to 350°F. Line a baking sheet with paper towels and set a cooling rack on top.

Fry the chicken in batches. Add 5 or 6 pieces of chicken at a time to the oil and cook for 3 to 4 minutes. Then flip the chicken and cook until golden brown and the juices run clear when pierced, 3 to 4 minutes more.

Remove to the prepared cooling rack and let sit for 5 minutes.

TO MAKE THE PANCAKES:
In a large bowl, combine the flour, sugar, baking powder, baking soda, and salt. In a medium bowl, whisk together the ricotta, milk, vanilla, and eggs. Add the wet ingredients to the dry ingredients and stir with a wooden spoon just until combined.

Preheat the oven to 175°F.

Heat about 1 tablespoon each vegetable oil and butter in a large cast-iron or nonstick skillet over medium heat. When the butter is foamy, reduce the heat to medium-low and ladle a heaping ¼ cup pancake batter into the skillet. Repeat to make 2 more pancakes. Cook until bubbles start to form in the batter and the pancakes are golden underneath, about 3 minutes. Flip and cook the other side until golden, another 3 minutes. Place the finished pancakes on a baking sheet and hold in the oven while you finish cooking the remaining batter, adding more oil and butter as necessary. Serve with the warm chicken strips and spicy syrup.

Fluffy French Toast with Peaches and Cream

Serves 3

1 cup milk

2 large eggs

¼ cup all-purpose flour

1 tablespoon granulated sugar

1 teaspoon almond extract

1 teaspoon vanilla extract

½ teaspoon ground cinnamon

½ teaspoon kosher salt

Unsalted butter, for cooking and serving

6 slices thick-cut brioche (or other thick-cut bread)

Confectioners' sugar, for sprinkling

3 fresh peaches, sliced

Whipped cream, for topping

Maple syrup, for serving

In a large, shallow bowl, whisk together the milk, eggs, flour, granulated sugar, almond extract, vanilla extract, cinnamon, and salt until smooth.

In a large skillet over medium heat, melt some butter.

Soak the bread in the egg mixture on both sides. Working in batches, cook the bread until golden brown, 3 to 4 minutes per side. Sprinkle with the confectioners' sugar. Top with the fresh peaches and a dollop of whipped cream. Serve with maple syrup and butter.

Crispy Home Fries and Peppers

Serves 4 to 6

2 tablespoons kosher salt

2 pounds Yukon gold potatoes, scrubbed and diced into ¾-inch cubes

2 tablespoons cornstarch

1 tablespoon Miss Brown's House Seasoning (page 33)

Vegetable oil, for pan frying

1 red bell pepper, diced

1 green bell pepper, diced

1 yellow onion, diced

In a large pot over high heat, bring 2 quarts water and the salt to a boil. Add the potatoes, bring the water back to a boil, and cook, about 5 minutes. The potatoes will be soft on the outside while still firm in the center. Drain in a colander and transfer to a large bowl. Toss with the cornstarch and House Seasoning.

Heat a large, heavy-bottom skillet over medium-high heat. Add enough oil to coat the pan. Working in small batches, add the potatoes, red and green peppers, and onion to the hot oil, stirring and flipping constantly until the potatoes are golden brown on all sides, 6 to 7 minutes. Remove to a plate and repeat with the remaining potatoes and vegetables.

Candied Bacon

Makes 12 slices

Nonstick cooking spray
1 pound thick-cut bacon
⅓ cup sorghum or molasses

½ cup packed light brown sugar
1 tablespoon freshly ground black pepper

Preheat the oven to 375°F. Line a rimmed baking sheet with aluminum foil and place a wire rack on top. Coat the wire rack with nonstick cooking spray.

Arrange the bacon slices on the wire rack in a single layer. Brush the bacon slices with half of the sorghum or molasses. Sprinkle with half of the sugar and half of the pepper, pressing to adhere them to the sorghum. Turn the bacon over and repeat the process with the remaining sorghum, sugar, and pepper. Bake for 20 to 25 minutes or until bacon is fully cooked.

Remove the bacon from the oven and let it stand 5 minutes. (The bacon will crisp as it stands.)

Hash Brown Casserole

1 tablespoon unsalted butter, at room temperature

1 16-ounce bag frozen shredded hash brown potatoes, thawed

8 ounces sharp yellow cheddar cheese, shredded (about 4 cups), divided

½ cup sour cream, plus more for garnish

1 medium yellow onion, coarsely grated

Meat options:

6 slices bacon, cooked and chopped

8 ounces pork or turkey sausage, crumbled and cooked

1 cup cubed ham

1 large egg

1 ½ teaspoons sweet paprika

¼ teaspoon cayenne pepper

¼ cup plus 2 tablespoons chopped fresh chives, divided

Kosher salt

Freshly ground black pepper

Preheat the oven to 400°F. Grease a 9 × 9-inch casserole dish with the butter and set aside.

In a large bowl, put the hash browns, about 3 ½ cups of the cheddar, the sour cream, onion, egg, paprika, and cayenne, and ¼ cup of the chives. Season with salt and pepper and add meat, if using. Stir until combined. Pour into the prepared casserole dish and top with the remaining ½ cup of cheddar.

Bake until the casserole is heated through, the top is browned, and the sides are crispy, about 45 minutes. Let cool for 5 minutes. Cut into slices and dollop with more sour cream and the remaining 2 tablespoons of chives.

Fancy BLT with Pickled Red Onions

Make the pickled red onions and the Easy Garlic Herb Aioli ahead of time.

Serves 2

For the pickled red onions

1 large red onion, thinly sliced

1 tablespoon pickling spice

1 cup red wine vinegar (or vinegar of your choice)

1 cup water

1 tablespoon kosher salt

1 tablespoon sugar

For the Easy Garlic Herb Aioli

1 cup mayonnaise

1 teaspoon garlic powder

1 teaspoon Italian seasoning

Kosher salt

Freshly ground black pepper

For the BLTs

8 slices thick-cut bacon (preferably applewood-smoked)

4 slices thick-cut artisan bread (or your favorite bread), toasted

2 firm beefsteak tomatoes, sliced

Kosher salt

Freshly ground black pepper

4 leaves of iceberg or butter lettuce, cleaned

TO MAKE THE PICKLED RED ONIONS:

Pack the onion into a 16-ounce mason jar. Add the pickling spice. In a medium saucepan, heat the vinegar, water, salt, and sugar over medium heat. Stir until the salt and sugar dissolve, about 1 minute. Cool about 5 minutes, then pour over the onion. Set aside to cool to room temperature for at least 1 hour, then cover and refrigerate until ready to use.

TO MAKE THE EASY GARLIC HERB AIOLI:

Combine the mayonnaise, garlic powder, and Italian seasoning in a small bowl. Season to taste with salt and pepper. Cover and refrigerate until ready to use.

TO MAKE THE BLTS:

Preheat the oven to 425°F. Line a baking sheet with parchment paper and place the bacon evenly on the sheet. Bake 8 to 9 minutes, or until crispy. Remove the bacon from the oven and transfer to a wire rack or paper towels to remove excess oil.

Spread the garlic aioli over each slice of bread. For each sandwich, layer 4 slices of bacon and half of the tomatoes on a piece of bread, sprinkle with salt and pepper to taste, and add 2 leaves of the lettuce and some pickled red onions. Top with the remaining bread, cut lengthwise, and serve.

Smoked Sausage and Egg Skillet

Serves 4	

8 ounces medium shrimp, peeled and deveined

2 ½ teaspoons Miss Brown's House Seasoning (page 33)

2 tablespoons unsalted butter

½ medium onion, chopped

½ medium green bell pepper, seeded and chopped

½ medium red bell pepper, seeded and chopped

6 ounces andouille sausage, sliced ¼-inch thick

1 clove garlic, minced

6 large eggs, beaten

¼ cup whole milk

½ cup shredded white cheddar cheese

2 tablespoons thinly sliced scallions

Preheat the broiler. Toss the shrimp with the House Seasoning in a small bowl and set aside.

In a large cast-iron skillet over medium heat, melt the butter. Add the onion and green and red peppers and cook, stirring occasionally, until the onions begin to turn translucent, about 5 minutes. Add the shrimp, andouille, and garlic and cook, stirring constantly, until the shrimp are opaque and the sausage is heated through, about 2 minutes.

Whisk the eggs and milk together then slowly scramble the mixture with a silicone spatula, scraping up large curds from the bottom of the pan. As soon as the eggs are almost set, but still a tiny bit runny (about 2 minutes), remove from the heat and sprinkle with the cheddar.

Broil until the cheese melts, 10 to 15 seconds. Remove the skillet from the oven and sprinkle with the scallions.

Crab Cake Scrambled Benedict with Old Bay Hollandaise

For the crab cakes

1 large egg, lightly beaten

¼ cup mayonnaise

2 teaspoons Dijon mustard

1 teaspoon Worcestershire sauce

1 teaspoon seafood seasoning,
such as Old Bay

17 butter crackers, such as Ritz, crushed
(about ⅔ cup crumbs)

8 ounces fresh jumbo lump crabmeat,
picked for shells

2 tablespoons canola or vegetable oil

For the hollandaise

8 tablespoons (1 stick) unsalted butter

3 large egg yolks

1 teaspoon freshly squeezed lemon juice

2 heavy pinches of Old Bay Seasoning

For the scramble

2 tablespoons unsalted butter

4 large eggs, lightly beaten with 2 teaspoons
whole milk

2 English muffins, halved and toasted

Scallions, for garnish (optional)

TO MAKE THE CRAB CAKES:

In a large bowl, mix together the egg, mayonnaise, mustard, Worcestershire sauce, and seafood seasoning. Fold in the cracker crumbs and crabmeat until just combined, being careful not to break up the crab too much. Shape the mixture into 4 patties, trying to make straight sides and flat bottoms. Cover and refrigerate until firm, about 1 hour.

Preheat the oven to 200°F.

Heat the oil in a large cast-iron skillet over medium-high heat. Place the crab cakes in the pan, making sure not to overcrowd the pan. Cook until golden brown, 2 to 3 minutes on each side. Transfer the crab cakes to a plate and hold in the warm oven until ready to serve.

TO MAKE THE HOLLANDAISE:

Melt the butter in a small saucepan and set aside. In a food processor or blender, add the egg yolks, lemon juice, and Old Bay seasoning and blend to combine. While the processor is running, slowly pour the melted butter down the chute. Turn off the processor once the butter is emulsified (fully incorporated) into the egg yolk mixture. Allow the sauce to cool slightly and thicken. This will take about 3 to 4 minutes.

TO MAKE THE SCRAMBLE:

In a small skillet over medium heat, melt the butter, then add the eggs. Scramble gently with a wooden spoon and remove from the heat when done to your liking. Set aside.

Place an English muffin half on each plate. Place a crab cake on top of each muffin half, add the scrambled eggs and hollandaise sauce, and top with the scallions, if using.

NOTE: *For a thicker sauce, heat it over a water bath on the stove or let it stand in a bowl until it reaches the desired thickness.*

Field Greens and Egg Frittata

Serves 8 to 10

4 tablespoons (½ stick) unsalted butter, at room temperature, divided

3 cups chopped mustard greens

1 clove garlic, minced

Kosher salt

Freshly ground black pepper

12 large eggs

½ cup milk

½ cup baking mix, preferably Bisquick

2 cups grated sharp yellow cheddar cheese

2 cups grated Monterey Jack cheese

2 cups frozen hash browns

Preheat the oven to 350°F. Grease a 9 × 13-inch baking dish with 1 tablespoon of the butter.

Melt the remaining 3 tablespoons of butter in a skillet over medium heat. Add the mustard greens, garlic, and a pinch of salt and pepper and sauté just until wilted, 2 to 3 minutes. Remove from the heat and cool slightly.

In a large bowl, whisk together the eggs, milk, baking mix, ½ teaspoon salt, and some pepper until well incorporated. Stir in the mustard greens, cheddar and Monterey Jack cheeses, and hash browns. Pour into the greased baking dish. Bake until puffed lightly, golden brown, and soft-set in the middle, 45 to 50 minutes. Cool slightly before slicing. Serve warm.

Black Cherry Muffins with Cornmeal Streusel

For the streusel topping

¼ cup finely chopped pecans

½ cup packed light brown sugar

¼ cup all-purpose flour

⅓ cup cornmeal

3 tablespoons unsalted butter, melted

For the muffins

2 large eggs, at room temperature

1 cup granulated sugar

1 cup sour cream, at room temperature

½ cup vegetable oil

1 tablespoon grated orange peel

2 teaspoons vanilla extract

2 cups plus 1 teaspoon all-purpose flour, divided

1 teaspoon baking powder

¼ teaspoon baking soda

½ teaspoon kosher salt

1½ cups whole frozen pitted cherries, thawed

TO MAKE THE STREUSEL TOPPING:

In a small bowl, combine the pecans, brown sugar, flour, cornmeal, and butter. Set aside.

TO MAKE THE MUFFINS:

Preheat the oven to 375°F. Line a standard muffin tin with cupcake liners.

In the bowl of a stand mixer, or in a large bowl with a hand mixer, beat together the eggs and granulated sugar on high speed for 4 to 5 minutes, until pale in color.

Add the sour cream, vegetable oil, orange peel, and vanilla. Beat on low speed until combined, about 30 seconds.

In a medium bowl, whisk together 2 cups of the flour, the baking powder, baking soda, and salt. Add the flour mixture to the wet ingredients in three batches, mixing on low speed until each addition is incorporated. Avoid overmixing, as this will result in dense, undesirable muffins.

In a small bowl, toss the cherries with the remaining 1 teaspoon of flour to coat. Use a spatula to gently fold the cherries into the batter just until combined.

Using an ice cream scooper, scoop the batter equally into the muffin tin, filling each cup about three-quarters full. Evenly distribute the streusel topping on top of the batter. Bake until the muffin tops are slightly golden and a toothpick inserted into the center comes out clean, 25 to 30 minutes. (If using frozen cherries, the time may increase by 10 minutes.)

Let the muffins cool in the muffin tin for 5 minutes, then transfer onto a cooling rack until ready to enjoy.

Fried "Fush" and Grits

For marinating the fish

¼ cup whole milk

Miss Brown's House Seasoning (page 33)

4 small catfish fillets, about 4 ounces each

For the grits

1 cup stone-ground grits (or quick grits if short on time)

2 cups half-and-half, or more if needed

4 tablespoons (½ stick) unsalted butter

Kosher salt

Freshly ground black pepper

For cooking the fish

Vegetable oil, for frying

1 cup finely ground yellow cornmeal

¼ cup all-purpose flour

Miss Brown's House Seasoning (page 33)

Unsalted butter, for serving

Hot sauce, for serving (optional)

TO MARINATE THE FISH:

In a small bowl, combine the milk and 1 generous pinch of House Seasoning. Pour the milk mixture into a shallow baking dish large enough to hold the fillets. Spread the fillets in an even layer in the dish, turning to coat each side. Let marinate for about 1 hour in a cool place or in the refrigerator.

TO MAKE THE GRITS:

In a medium saucepan over medium-high heat, bring 2 cups water to a boil and add the grits slowly, stirring with a whisk. Cover and reduce the heat to low, stirring often as the grits thicken. Whisk in the half-and-half, butter, and a pinch of salt and pepper. Continue to cook and whisk often for about 30 minutes. (If you're in a crunch for time, you can use 5-minute quick grits instead.)

TO COOK THE FISH:

Pour 2 inches of oil into a large Dutch oven over medium high heat. Heat until oil reaches between 350 and 375°F. Add a tiny pinch of cornmeal to the pot; if it starts to sizzle and rises to the top, your oil is ready to go! My momma taught me this.

(cont.)

Meanwhile, in a small bowl, stir together the cornmeal, flour, and a pinch of House Seasoning, then transfer to a clean paper lunch bag. Working with a few fillets at a time, remove them from the marinade, allowing any excess to drip off. Place them in the paper bag and gently turn the bag over several times until the fillets are evenly coated with the cornmeal mixture. Transfer the coated fillets to a baking sheet while you repeat the process with the remaining fillets.

Working in batches, fry the fillets about 5 minutes, or until golden brown and crisp on the outside and moist and flaky inside, adjusting the heat to maintain temperature. Transfer them to a clean wire rack set over a rimmed baking sheet to drain. Place ladlefuls of grits on deep plates, place the fillets on top, and serve with butter and, if you'd like, a little hot sauce.

Homemade Breakfast Sausage

Makes 10 to 12 patties

2 pounds ground pork

2 tablespoons packed dark brown sugar

2 teaspoons rubbed sage

2 teaspoons kosher salt

½ teaspoon garlic powder

½ teaspoon smoked paprika

½ teaspoon freshly ground black pepper

Pinch of crushed red pepper flakes

2 tablespoons unsalted butter

Put the pork in a large bowl and add the brown sugar, sage, salt, garlic powder, paprika, black pepper, and red pepper flakes. Mix well with your hands. Form patties about ⅓-inch thick, using a heaping ¼ cup of the mixture for each one.

Melt the butter in a large cast-iron skillet over medium-high heat. Cook the sausage patties in two batches until the internal temperature reaches 160°F, about 5 minutes per side. Serve warm with eggs or pancakes (see Note).

NOTE: *Sausage patties can be cooked, cooled, and then frozen. Thaw and reheat in the microwave or on the stovetop in a skillet over medium heat.*

Preserving

Nowadays the food I grew up on

is called "farm-to-table." The Sea Islands area, at its core, is focused on the natural freshness of eating from the land. That's why preserving is second nature for us. My grandmother taught me, of course. Back in the day, think about it—most people didn't have the luxury of refrigeration. So underneath the house the Mason jars went with their scrumptious contents. People would preserve pears, okra, and other fruits and vegetables they loved to eat throughout the year.

The beauty of preserving is that you not only get to enjoy the tastes 365 days a year—you also get to enjoy the textures. Believe me, the delicious cabbage and bell peppers in your chowchow will still have the fresh snap in your mouth. A lot of the tasty things that are considered staples of southern cooking come directly from the preserving techniques used to keep food from going bad before it was eaten up.

You take okra, for example. In hot weather it grows superfast, and it needs to be harvested every couple of days. Cousins, you know I love me some okra. But even I can't eat it that fast. The same with cucumbers. You don't know what you're missing if you've never experienced the tart deliciousness of fresh pickles.

Now, don't be scuurred. Preserving is really super simple and fun. I know no one really does a whole lot of it these days. But the flavor can't be beat.

Some of the sweet and sour flavors that I like so much for the way they play off one another were actually introduced to the US by West African enslaved people—who also, by the way, brought their skills of drying and salting fish. I want to introduce you here to some of my favorite preserving recipes ever. Try one and I promise you'll be hooked!

Quick Pickled Okra

For this recipe, you'll need two 1-quart canning jars with lids or four pint-size jars. Be sure to sterilize them in boiling water before use.

Makes 2 quarts

---

1 ½ cups white distilled vinegar
1 cup sugar
3 tablespoons kosher salt
2 teaspoons ground turmeric

1 ½ pounds fresh okra
1 large white onion, thinly sliced
½ cup pickling spices

Put the vinegar, sugar, salt, and turmeric in a medium saucepan with 3 cups water. Bring to a boil and stir until the sugar and salt dissolve, then reduce the heat to low and keep warm.

Divide the okra and onion among the sterilized jars. Evenly distribute the pickling spices among the jars. Slowly add the sweet vinegar water, seal the jars with lids, and refrigerate. The okra can be enjoyed right away but will improve in flavor after several days and will keep in the refrigerator for about 4 to 6 months.

Sweet and Spicy Southern Chowchow

For this recipe, you'll need two 1-quart canning jars with lids or four pint-size jars.
Be sure to sterilize them in boiling water before use. Please use gloves while handling jalapeños.

Makes 2 quarts

5 cups white distilled vinegar
3 cups granulated sugar
2 tablespoons kosher salt
1 tablespoon whole cloves
1 tablespoon mustard seeds
1 tablespoon whole black peppercorns
1 teaspoon yellow mustard powder
1 teaspoon ground turmeric
Pinch of crushed red pepper flakes

1 bay leaf
4 green tomatoes, finely diced
2 green bell peppers, finely diced
1 red bell pepper, finely diced
1 jalapeño pepper, seeded and finely diced
1 large sweet onion, such as Vidalia, finely diced
½ head cabbage, shredded (about 6 cups)

Put the vinegar, sugar, salt, cloves, mustard seeds, peppercorns, mustard powder, turmeric, red pepper flakes, and bay leaf in a large saucepan. Bring to a simmer over medium heat and cook, stirring occasionally, until the sugar dissolves and the flavors start to marry, about 5 minutes.

Add the tomatoes, green and red bell peppers, jalapeño pepper, onion, and cabbage and bring to a boil. Lower the heat to a simmer, stirring occasionally, for 15 to 20 minutes. Remove from the heat. Divide the mixture between the two jars and let cool to room temperature. Serve immediately or seal and refrigerate for up to 6 weeks.

Miss Brown's Pickles

For this recipe, you'll need three 1-quart canning jars with lids.
Be sure to sterilize them in boiling water before use.

Makes 3 quarts

1 ½ cups white vinegar
1 cup sugar
3 tablespoons kosher salt
2 teaspoons turmeric powder

3 cups sliced garden or store-bought cucumbers
1 large white onion, thinly sliced
3 cloves garlic, minced
½ cup pickling spices

Put the vinegar, sugar, salt, and turmeric in a medium saucepan with 3 cups water. Bring to a boil and stir until the sugar and salt dissolve, then reduce the heat to low and keep warm.

Divide the cucumbers, onion, and garlic among three 1-quart sterilized jars. Evenly distribute the pickling spices among the jars. Slowly add the sweet vinegar water, seal the jars with lids, and refrigerate. These pickles can be enjoyed right away but improve in flavor after several days.

Bacon Jam

For this recipe, you'll need one pint-size canning jar with a lid.

Be sure to sterilize it in boiling water before use.

Makes 1 pint

---

1 pound bacon

½ cup packed dark brown sugar

½ cup molasses

½ cup honey

¼ cup apple cider vinegar

¼ cup sherry

2 teaspoons garlic powder

1 teaspoon dry mustard powder

3 shallots, minced

3 cloves garlic, minced

Cook the bacon in a skillet over medium heat until crispy, about 5 minutes. Transfer the bacon to a cutting board, reserving 2 tablespoons of the bacon fat in the skillet. Chop the bacon into small pieces, then put it back in the skillet over medium-high heat.

Add the brown sugar, molasses, honey, vinegar, sherry, garlic powder, mustard powder, shallots, and garlic and bring the mixture to a slight boil. Reduce the heat to a simmer and cook until syrupy, 30 to 45 minutes. Let cool, then transfer to a canning jar and refrigerate. Enjoy within two days.

Hot Peppa Jelly

For this recipe, you'll need six half-pint (8-ounce) canning jars with lids.

Be sure to sterilize them in boiling water before use. Please use gloves while handling jalapeños.

Makes 48 ounces

---

1 large green bell pepper, coarsely chopped

1 large red bell pepper, coarsely chopped

8 jalapeño peppers, coarsely chopped

1 ½ cups white vinegar

5 cups sugar

2 3-ounce pouches liquid fruit pectin

2 teaspoons red beetroot powder or 2 drops of red food coloring (optional)

Place the green and red bell peppers and the jalapeños in a food processor and give it a few pulses. In a large pot, add the peppers, vinegar, and sugar; bring to a boil, stirring constantly. Stir in the pectin and beetroot powder, if using. Continue to boil 1 minute, stirring constantly. Remove from the heat and skim off the foam.

Ladle the hot mixture into six hot, sterilized half-pint jars, leaving a little headspace. Wipe the rims. Add the lids and tightly secure. Place the jars in a hot water bath for 5 minutes to process. Store in the fridge if the lid pops back. If the lid does not pop back, it is safe to keep the jar at room temperature.

Great-Grandma's Preserved Pears

For this recipe, you'll need a canning funnel, jar-lifting tongs, and three 16-ounce wide-mouth canning jars with lids. Be sure to sterilize the jars in boiling water before use.

Makes 48 ounces

Juice of 1 lemon

3 quarts water, divided

6 pounds Bartlett pears

2 cups sugar

3 vanilla beans

In a very large bowl, combine the lemon juice and 2 quarts of the water. Peel and trim each pear, then add it to the lemon water to prevent it from oxidizing. In a large saucepan, add the lemon, the remaining 1 quart of water, and the sugar. Bring to a boil and stir to dissolve the sugar. Add the pears to the boiling water. Return to a boil and cook for about 5 minutes. Using a canning funnel, pack the pears into the wide-mouth canning jars and discard the lemon. Add 1 vanilla bean to each jar. Pour the sugar water over the pears to just cover them. Do not overfill. Tightly secure a lid on top of each jar. For shelf life, put the jars in a boiling water bath for 20 minutes. Using jar-lifter tongs, remove the jars from the pot and gently set them aside to cool on a towel or rack. Let them rest overnight on your countertop. Store at room temperature or in the fridge for up to 1 year. My great-grandmother stored her canned fruit in a root cellar.

Strawberry Balsamic Jam

For this recipe, you'll need one 16-ounce canning jar with a lid or two 8-ounce canning jars.
Be sure to sterilize them in boiling water before use.

Makes 16 ounces

---

2 pounds very ripe strawberries, washed, stems removed, and halved

1 cup sugar

2 teaspoons vanilla extract

1 tablespoon balsamic vinegar

1 teaspoon freshly squeezed lemon juice

Zest of ½ lemon

Preheat the oven to 350°F.

In a large bowl, toss the strawberries with the sugar, vanilla, and vinegar. Transfer the strawberry mixture to a ceramic baking dish. Roast uncovered for 60 minutes or until the mixture is thick and syrupy. Check during the last 15 minutes of cooking to make sure the sugar is not burning.

Remove from the oven and allow to cool. Stir in the lemon juice and lemon zest. Transfer to the canning jar. Store in the refrigerator for up to thirty days.

Serve the jam on toast or biscuits or eat it straight out of the jar with a spoon.

Main Dishes

Psssst. Cousins, allow me to clear the air right quick. Not all soul food goodness is rich and swimming in meat or butter, okay? Pass it on!

You know that old saying, "You don't know what you don't know"? Well, that's me. I grew up eating such a wide variety of good food in Charleston and on Wadmalaw Island that I had no idea how some folks perceived southern cooking till I was a full-grown woman. I learned that while most everyone loves our great dishes, a lot of people think it begins with fried chicken and ends with gravy.

Nothing could be further from the truth! What you will see in this chapter is the vast range of what our food is really about. It can't be pigeonholed or marginalized. All the main dishes I've come to love are hearty, but who says hearty has to be heavy?

If you follow me on social media, know that—even if I can't respond to each of your comments—I *am* reading them. And what I know is that the most popular posts—the ones liked, loved, and commented on—are hands-down comfort-food favorites. To me, if there is one common thread throughout these dishes, it's that. Y'all, the entrees I've selected here are some of my favorites, because they simply make you *feel* good. Several can be made in just one pot. And the best part is, those that can't still won't have you tied to the stove all day.

Yes, you can make the baked ribs on a weeknight. Some of my best memories growing up are Ma and me across the dinner table on a regular evening. I mean, of course I loved holidays and special occasion meals. But nothing compares to the ease and simple joy of sitting down with Ma after school—when homework and practice were over—and eating something like her stuffed burgers. They were juicy, a bit spicy, and slightly tangy, with a just-right mix of garlic and chives. Filling up with all the love she'd put into a meal like that made everything that may have been wrong about the day suddenly seem all right.

Lowcountry Spatchcocked Chicken

1 cup packed fresh parsley leaves

8 tablespoons (1 stick) salted butter, softened

3 tablespoons freshly squeezed lemon juice

1 tablespoon fresh oregano leaves or 2 teaspoons dried

1 tablespoon dry sherry

½ teaspoon crushed red pepper flakes

2 cloves garlic, peeled and smashed

2 fresh sprigs thyme, stems removed

1 teaspoon kosher salt

1 teaspoon freshly ground black pepper

1 5-pound whole chicken

Preheat the oven to 450°F.

In a food processor, pulse the parsley, butter, lemon juice, oregano, sherry, red pepper flakes, garlic, thyme leaves, salt, and pepper until well combined. Scrape the mixture into a small dish and set aside. Do not refrigerate.

Place the chicken, breast-side down, on a cutting board. Using a chef's knife or kitchen shears, cut along one side of the backbone. Repeat on the other side and remove the backbone completely. (Save it for stock!) Turn the chicken over and press down on the breastbone with the heel of your hand until it cracks. Place the chicken on a rimmed baking sheet and tuck the wing tips under the chicken so they don't burn.

Rub half of the butter mixture under the skin of the breasts and thighs of the chicken. Melt the remaining butter mixture in a pan on the stovetop or in the microwave and brush it all over the chicken.

Cover the chicken with foil and bake for 20 minutes. Uncover and baste with any remaining butter or cooking liquid on the bottom of the pan. Continue to bake until the chicken is dark brown with an internal temperature of 165 to 170°F on an instant-read thermometer, 40 to 45 minutes more.

Jerk Chicken Rasta Pasta

Serves 3 to 4 (14 cups)

---

16 ounces penne pasta

1 ½ pounds boneless, skinless chicken breast

3 teaspoons jerk seasoning, divided

2 teaspoons unpacked light brown sugar

Canola, vegetable, or other neutral oil, for frying

1 green bell pepper, sliced

1 red bell pepper, sliced

2 tablespoons unsalted butter

2 large cloves garlic, minced

1 1.3-ounce packet Knorr Parma Rosa Sauce Mix (see Note)

1 tablespoon all-purpose flour

2 cups half-and-half

1 cup grated Parmesan cheese, plus extra for serving

Kosher salt

Freshly ground black pepper

1 scallion, sliced, for garnish

Prepare the pasta according to package directions; drain and rinse with cold water, then set aside.

Slice the chicken breast into strips. Sprinkle with 2 teaspoons of the jerk seasoning and the brown sugar.

Pour enough oil in a large, deep cast-iron or other skillet to just cover the bottom. Heat to medium-high. Add the green and red peppers and chicken and cook for 8 to 10 minutes, turning occasionally. When done, remove the skillet from the heat and set aside.

In a saucepan over medium-high heat, melt the butter. Add the garlic and cook just until it softens. Add the sauce packet and flour, mixing with a wooden spoon until incorporated. Reduce the heat to low and slowly add the half-and-half. Whisk out any lumps from the flour and butter. Raise the heat to a gentle simmer and cook for 3 to 4 minutes, or until the mixture begins to thicken. Remove from the heat and stir in the Parmesan, the remaining 1 teaspoon of jerk seasoning, and a heavy pinch of salt and pepper. Add the sauce to the skillet with the chicken and peppers. Then add the cooked pasta and toss until fully incorporated.

Garnish with the scallion slices. Serve warm with extra Parmesan.

NOTE: *This sauce mix can be ordered online if you can't find it in the supermarket.*

Fried Pork Chops

Serves 4

1 ½ cups buttermilk

1 ½ cups all-purpose flour

2 tablespoons Miss Brown's House Seasoning (page 33), divided

1 tablespoon hot sauce, plus more for serving

1 teaspoon yellow mustard

4 thin bone-in pork-loin chops (about 2 pounds total)

Canola oil, for frying

Pour the buttermilk into a shallow baking dish and set aside. In another shallow baking dish, stir together the flour and 1 tablespoon plus 2 teaspoons of the House Seasoning, and set aside.

In a small bowl, stir together the hot sauce, mustard, and the remaining 1 teaspoon of House Seasoning. Rub the seasoning mix onto both sides of the pork chops. Place the pork chops in the buttermilk and turn to coat completely.

Pour 1 inch of oil into a large cast-iron skillet. Heat over medium-high heat until a deep-fry thermometer reaches 350°F.

Working with one piece at a time, remove the pork chops from the buttermilk, letting any excess drip off. Coat in the flour mixture and carefully add to the hot oil. Fry, turning once, until the chops are browned and reach an internal temperature of 150°F, about 4 minutes per side. Transfer to a clean wire rack set over a rimmed baking sheet to drain.

Serve hot with white bread and hot sauce or your favorite sides.

Lowcountry Cheesesteak with Have Mercy Sauce

Serves 4

For the cheesesteak

1 pound lump crabmeat, drained and picked for shells

1 ½ teaspoons seafood seasoning, such as Old Bay

3 tablespoons unsalted butter, divided, plus more if needed

2 large yellow onions, thinly sliced

2 tablespoons soy sauce, divided

2 tablespoons Worcestershire sauce, divided

1 pound thinly shaved beef

Kosher salt

Freshly ground black pepper

½ cup chopped jarred cherry peppers

4 thick slices American cheese

4 Italian hoagie rolls, split

For the Have Mercy Sauce

1 cup mayonnaise

⅓ cup Dijon mustard

2 tablespoons dill pickle brine

2 tablespoons hot sauce

2 teaspoons seafood seasoning, such as Old Bay

TO MAKE THE CHEESESTEAK:

In a medium bowl, gently toss together the crabmeat and seafood seasoning, then refrigerate.

Melt 2 tablespoons of the butter on a griddle or in a large skillet over medium heat. Add the onion, 1 tablespoon of the soy sauce, and 1 tablespoon of the Worcestershire sauce and cook until the onion starts to soften, about 5 minutes. Raise the heat to high, add the beef, and cook, adding more butter if needed and breaking up the meat with a spatula. Stir in the remaining 1 tablespoon of soy sauce and 1 tablespoon of Worcestershire sauce, sprinkle with salt and pepper, and continue to cook until the beef is no longer pink, about 2 minutes.

Stir in the cherry peppers. Push the beef and onions over to the side of the griddle and cover with the cheese slices. Melt the remaining 1 tablespoon of butter in the cleared area of the griddle, add the crabmeat, and cook just until warmed through, about 2 minutes.

Spread both halves of the rolls with the Have Mercy Sauce. Spoon the beef and onion mixture and crabmeat into the rolls.

TO MAKE THE HAVE MERCY SAUCE:

Stir together the mayonnaise, mustard, pickle brine, hot sauce, and seafood seasoning in a small bowl until smooth. The sauce keeps, refrigerated in an airtight container, for up to a week.

Gullah Gumbo

1 cup vegetable oil

1 cup all-purpose flour

1 ½ cups chopped onion

1 cup chopped celery

1 cup chopped green pepper

1 pound sliced smoked meat (I use smoked sausage)

Kosher salt

Freshly ground black pepper

1 teaspoon ground ginger

1 tablespoon filé powder*

2 tablespoons minced garlic

2 bay leaves

3 cups shrimp broth or fish stock

3 cups chicken broth

1 cup water, plus more if needed

1 14.5-ounce can diced tomatoes (do not drain)

1 pound fresh or frozen okra, sliced

8 ounces canned baby lima beans

1 pound medium-large shrimp, peeled and deveined

1 pound crab claw meat, picked for shells

2 tablespoons chopped fresh parsley leaves, plus more for topping

½ cup chopped scallions, plus more for topping

Steamed white rice, for serving

Fresh herbs for garnish, such as rosemary, thyme, tarragon, and sage

Combine the oil and flour in a Dutch oven over medium heat. To make a light- to medium-brown roux, stir constantly for 10 to 15 minutes. Add the onion, celery, and bell pepper and cook, stirring for 4 to 5 minutes until transparent. Add the smoked meat with a heavy pinch of salt, a heavy pinch of pepper, ginger, filé powder, garlic, and bay leaves. Stir for another 2 to 3 minutes. Slowly add the shrimp broth, chicken broth, water, and tomatoes with their juices to the pot. Using a large whisk, whisk until the roux mixture and the liquids are well combined. Bring to a boil, then reduce the heat to medium-low. Cook, uncovered and stirring occasionally, for 1 hour. Add more water as needed.

Turn the heat down to medium and add the okra and lima beans. Cover the pot and simmer for 2 hours. During the last 10 minutes of cooking, add the shrimp and crabmeat. Remove from the heat. Stir in the parsley and scallions and remove the bay leaves. Top with additional chopped parsley and scallions. Serve with white rice. Garnish with fresh rosemary, thyme, tarragon, and sage.

Dried and ground leaves of the sassafras tree. It is a very popular ingredient in Cajun/Creole cooking.

Carolina Smoky Baked Ribs

For the ribs

½ cup soy sauce
½ cup Worcestershire sauce
1 tablespoon liquid smoke

1 ½ tablespoons BBQ rub (I prefer a rub with brown sugar)
Pinch of kosher salt
1 ½ teaspoons freshly ground black pepper
1 rack of spare ribs (about 4 pounds)

For the tangy Carolina BBQ sauce

1 ½ cups yellow mustard
1 cup sugar
½ cup molasses
½ cup apple cider vinegar
2 teaspoons Worcestershire sauce
2 heaping teaspoons garlic powder

2 heaping teaspoons onion powder
½ teaspoon smoked paprika
A few dashes of hot sauce
Kosher salt
Freshly ground black pepper

TO MAKE THE RIBS:

In a large measuring cup, mix together the soy sauce, Worcestershire sauce, liquid smoke, BBQ rub, salt, and pepper. Place the ribs in a roasting pan, hotel pan, or large baking dish. Pour the marinade over the ribs. Toss and flip the ribs until they are coated. Marinate 1 hour at room temperature or refrigerate up to overnight.

Preheat the oven to 250°F. Line a rimmed baking sheet with aluminum foil.

Transfer the ribs to the baking sheet, meat-side up. Brush with any marinade left in the roasting pan. Cover with more foil. Bake for 2 hours.

TO MAKE THE TANGY CAROLINA BBQ SAUCE:

Meanwhile, in a medium saucepan, mix together the mustard, sugar, molasses, vinegar, Worcestershire sauce, garlic powder, onion powder, paprika, and hot sauce. Season lightly with salt and pepper. Bring to a boil over medium-high heat. Reduce to medium-low and simmer until thickened, about 1 hour.

Uncover the ribs and drain off the fat. Brush the sauce on both sides, returning the ribs to meat-side up. Raise the oven to 300°F and bake the ribs, uncovered, until the meat is tender and the sauce begins to caramelize, about 1 more hour.

Brush the ribs with the sauce again on both sides. Raise the oven temperature to 375°F and bake the ribs, uncovered and adding more sauce as it get absorbed, until the meat becomes brown and caramelized, about 1 hour more. Cut the ribs into individual pieces. Use the remaining sauce for serving or keep it in the refrigerator for later use.

Southern Smothered Chicken

Serve with rice and broccoli.

Serves 4

1 cup all-purpose flour

1 tablespoon Miss Brown's House Seasoning (page 33)

4 bone-in chicken thighs

Canola, vegetable, or other neutral oil, for frying

1 large onion, sliced

2 tablespoons unsalted butter

2 teaspoons garlic powder

1 teaspoon onion powder

2 teaspoons poultry seasoning

2 cups low-sodium chicken stock or broth

Kosher salt

Freshly ground black pepper

2 tablespoons chopped fresh parsley leaves

Whisk together the flour and House Seasoning in a large bowl. Add the chicken and toss to coat.

In a large cast-iron skillet over medium-high heat, heat enough oil to shallow-fry the chicken. Remove the chicken from the flour mixture, shaking to remove any excess, and add to the hot oil. (Reserve the extra flour for the sauce.) Fry until the chicken is golden brown on all sides, about 5 minutes per side. Transfer to a plate and set aside.

Pour off all but 2 tablespoons of oil. Add the sliced onion to the hot oil in the skillet and cook until the onion is slightly softened and translucent, 5 minutes. Add the butter, 3 tablespoons of the leftover flour, the garlic powder, onion powder, and poultry seasoning and cook until fragrant and browned, about 1 minute. Whisk in the stock, scraping up any bits from the bottom of the pan. Simmer until thickened, 3 to 4 minutes. Taste, then season with salt and pepper. Add the chicken, turning to coat with the gravy. Cover and cook, turning the chicken occasionally, 25 to 30 minutes. Sprinkle with the parsley before serving.

Sea Island Wings

Serves 6 to 8

1 cup hot sauce

½ cup molasses

4 tablespoons (½ stick) unsalted butter

2 tablespoons packed light brown sugar

1 tablespoon kosher salt

2 teaspoons garlic powder

2 teaspoons smoked paprika

2 teaspoons freshly ground black pepper

¾ cup olive oil, plus extra for oiling the grill

3 pounds whole chicken wings

½ cup thinly sliced scallions (cut on a bias), optional

2 tablespoons chopped fresh parsley leaves, optional

Preheat a grill or grill pan to medium-high heat.

Mix together the hot sauce, molasses, and butter in a small pot over medium heat. Cook until combined, about 3 minutes, then set aside.

Whisk together the brown sugar, salt, garlic powder, paprika, and pepper in a small bowl. Whisk the oil into the dry mixture, creating a loose rub. Set a quarter of the mixture aside to use for basting.

Slather the wings with the remaining rub. Brush the grill grates with a little olive oil, then place the wings on the grill. Cook, covered, for about 10 minutes, then baste with the reserved rub. Flip and baste with any remaining rub and cook for another 15 minutes. Transfer the wings from the grill to a large bowl and toss with the hot sauce mixture. Transfer to a platter and sprinkle with the scallions and parsley, if using.

Lowcountry Crab Cakes

Serves 6

1 large egg, lightly beaten

½ cup mayonnaise

1 tablespoon Dijon mustard

1 tablespoon Worcestershire sauce

2 teaspoons seafood seasoning, such as Old Bay

34 butter crackers, such as Ritz, crushed (about 1 cup)

1 pound fresh jumbo lump crabmeat, picked for shells

Vegetable oil, for frying

For the rémoulade

1 cup mayonnaise

¼ cup ketchup

2 tablespoons whole-grain mustard

1 tablespoon prepared horseradish

1 tablespoon freshly squeezed lemon juice

1 tablespoon chopped fresh chives

In a large bowl, mix together the egg, mayonnaise, mustard, Worcestershire sauce, and seafood seasoning. Fold in the cracker crumbs and crabmeat until just combined, being careful not to break up the crab too much. Shape the mixture into six 2- to 2 ½-inch patties, trying to make straight sides and flat bottoms. Cover and refrigerate until firm, about 1 hour.

Preheat the oven to 200°F.

Heat 2 tablespoons oil in a large cast-iron skillet over medium-high heat. Add the crab cakes in batches, making sure not to overcrowd the pan. Cook until golden brown, 2 to 3 minutes on each side. Remove the crab cakes to a plate or platter and hold in the warm oven until needed. Repeat with the remaining crab cakes, adding more oil if needed. Serve warm with the rémoulade.

TO MAKE THE RÉMOULADE:

Mix the mayonnaise, ketchup, mustard, horseradish, lemon juice, and chives in a bowl until combined.

Smoky Pimento Cheese Stuffed Burgers

Serves 4

For the pimento cheese

8 ounces extra sharp yellow cheddar cheese, shredded

4 ounces white cheddar cheese (preferably Vermont cheddar), shredded

8 ounces cream cheese, softened

4 ounces diced pimentos, drained and juice reserved

3 tablespoons mayonnaise

1 tablespoon finely chopped fresh chives

1 teaspoon garlic powder

½ teaspoon cayenne pepper

½ teaspoon smoked paprika

Kosher salt to taste

Freshly ground black pepper to taste

For the sauce

⅓ cup mayonnaise

⅓ cup BBQ sauce (I prefer a hickory BBQ sauce)

Kosher salt

Freshly ground black pepper

For the burgers

1 ½ pounds 80/20 angus ground beef

2 tablespoons Worcestershire sauce

1 large egg, lightly beaten

½ teaspoon kosher salt

½ teaspoon freshly ground black pepper

Vegetable oil, for oiling the grill

4 hamburger buns, buttered and toasted

Toppings for serving: grilled red onion, sliced tomato, pickles, and lettuce

TO MAKE THE PIMENTO CHEESE:

In a medium bowl, mix together the yellow cheddar, white cheddar, cream cheese, pimentos, and mayonnaise. Add the chives, garlic powder, cayenne, paprika, salt, and pepper and mix until thoroughly combined.

Place the cheese mixture on a sheet of plastic wrap and form into a log. Freeze for a few minutes or refrigerate up to overnight.

TO MAKE THE SAUCE:

Mix together the mayonnaise and BBQ sauce in a medium bowl. Season with salt and pepper.

TO MAKE THE BURGERS:

Preheat a grill to medium heat.

Using your hands, mix the ground beef, beaten egg and Worcestershire sauce in a bowl until completely combined. Divide the meat into eight portions and shape each into large thin patties. Cut four ½-inch slices off the pimento cheese log (reserve the rest for another use . . . snacking!). Place a pimento cheese slice on four of the patties and then top them with the remaining four patties, sealing the sides to enclose the cheese. Sprinkle salt and pepper on both sides of the patties right before placing on the grill.

Lightly oil the grill grates. Add the patties to the hot grill and cook until they reach an internal temperature of 160°F, about 4 minutes per side.

Spread the sauce on the buttered buns, add the patties, and top with grilled red onion, sliced tomato, pickles, and lettuce. Eat with lots of napkins.

Not My Momma's Chicken and Dumplings

Serves 4

For the chicken

6 tablespoons (¾ stick) unsalted butter, divided

6 boneless, skinless chicken thighs

Kosher salt

Freshly ground black pepper

1 medium yellow onion, diced

4 stalks celery, sliced ½-inch thick

4 medium carrots, sliced into ½-inch-thick rounds

2 tablespoons all-purpose flour

2 cloves garlic, chopped

6 cups chicken stock

1 bay leaf

1/2 bunch of fresh parsley leaves, roughly chopped, for serving

For the dumplings

1 cup all-purpose flour

1 teaspoon baking powder

½ teaspoon kosher salt

2 tablespoons vegetable shortening

⅔ cup buttermilk

Nonstick cooking spray, optional

TO MAKE THE CHICKEN:

Heat a large braiser or Dutch oven over medium-high heat and add 4 tablespoons of the butter. Sprinkle the chicken thighs with salt and pepper and add to the pan. Cook until golden, turning once, about 3 minutes per side. Transfer to a plate.

Add the remaining 2 tablespoons of butter, the onion, celery, and carrots and season with salt and pepper. Cook, stirring frequently and scraping up the brown bits that cling to the bottom of the pan with a wooden spoon, until the vegetables are coated in fat and slightly golden, about 3 minutes. Sprinkle with the flour and stir until the vegetables are coated. Add the garlic and cook until fragrant, about 30 seconds. Add the chicken stock, bay leaf, and browned chicken, along with any chicken juices at the bottom of the plate. Bring to a boil, lower to a simmer, cover, and cook until the chicken is tender and cooked through, about 45 minutes.

TO MAKE THE DUMPLINGS:

Whisk together the flour, baking powder, and salt in a large bowl. Using a fork, cut the shortening into the flour mixture. Slowly add the buttermilk, gently mixing to incorporate.

Remove the chicken from the pot and use two forks to shred it. When the chicken is ready, return it to the pot and use 2 spoons sprayed with cooking spray, if using, to add scoops of dumpling dough over the top of the stew, about 1 tablespoon each. Cover and simmer until the dumplings double in size, about 15 minutes. Remove from the heat, discard the bay leaf, and garnish with parsley.

My Famous Fried Fish Sandwich

Serves 4

For the tartar sauce

½ cup mayonnaise

3 ½ tablespoons dill pickle relish

1 ½ teaspoons capers

1 teaspoon dried dill

1 teaspoon freshly squeezed lemon juice

Pinch of kosher salt

Pinch of freshly ground black pepper

Pinch of sugar

¼ onion, diced

For the fish sandwich

1 tablespoon freshly squeezed lemon juice, plus more as desired

4 6-ounce boneless, skinless halibut fillets or steaks

⅓ cup milk

2 large eggs

1 teaspoon kosher salt, plus more as desired

1 teaspoon freshly ground black pepper

½ cup all-purpose flour

1 ½ cups panko breadcrumbs

½ tablespoon seafood seasoning, such as Old Bay

Vegetable or canola oil, for frying

4 potato buns

Unsalted butter

4 slices American cheese

TO MAKE THE TARTAR SAUCE:

Mix together the mayonnaise, relish, capers, dill, lemon juice, salt, pepper, sugar, and onion in a bowl and refrigerate.

TO MAKE THE FISH SANDWICH:

Sprinkle the lemon juice over the fish fillets. Combine the milk, eggs, salt, and pepper in a shallow bowl. Put the flour on a large plate. Combine the breadcrumbs and seafood seasoning on another plate.

In a large Dutch oven, heat 2 inches of oil to 350°F.

One at a time, dip the fish fillets into the flour, then the egg and milk mixture, then the breadcrumbs. Set on another plate or a small baking sheet. Place the fish in the oil, making sure not to overcrowd the pan. Fry the fish, turning once, for 3 to 4 minutes total. (If you are using the shallow-frying method, cook both sides until golden brown, 2 to 3 minutes each side.) Using tongs, transfer the fish to a plate lined with paper towels or a wire rack set in a baking sheet. (I like to hit my fish with a little salt and lemon juice while it's hot.)

Meanwhile, split the buns and toast them by melting the butter in a pan and cooking the buns in it or by buttering the buns and broiling them until slightly golden. On the bun bottoms, place the cheese and the fish, then spread the bun tops with tartar sauce.

Low 'n' Slow Bolognese

1 large onion

1 stalk celery

1 carrot, peeled

2 cloves garlic

Vegetable oil (enough to cover bottom of pot)

Kosher salt

Freshly ground black pepper

2½ pounds beef chuck

4 slices thick-cut bacon, diced into small cubes

1½ cups low-sodium beef broth, plus more as needed

1 cup whole milk

1 cup good-quality dry red wine (merlot or cabernet sauvignon)

3 tablespoons tomato paste

1 bay leaf

1 pound fresh pappardelle or dry rigatoni

½ cup finely grated Parmesan cheese, plus more for serving

Basil or parsley leaves, thinly sliced, for serving (optional)

Preheat the oven to 300°F.

In a food processor, pulse the onion, celery, carrot, and garlic until very finely chopped. Set aside.

Heat the oil in a large Dutch oven or large oven-safe pot over medium-high heat. Liberally sprinkle salt and pepper on both sides of the beef. Add the beef to the pot and sear until golden brown on both sides, about 4 to 5 minutes total. Transfer the beef to a plate. Add the bacon to the pot and cook until crispy. With a slotted spoon, transfer the bacon to a plate lined with paper towels, leaving the bacon grease in the pot.

Add more oil to the pot if needed and sauté the minced veggies and garlic until softened. Add the beef stock, milk, wine, and tomato paste. Stir, then taste and add salt and pepper to your liking. Return the beef and bacon to the pot. Add the bay leaf. Transfer the pot to the oven and bake for 2½ to 3 hours, until the sauce has thickened and the beef is super tender. Check midway and add a little beef broth if the sauce becomes dry. Remove the pot from the oven and discard the bay leaf. Shred the beef by using two forks to pull it apart. Place the pot on the stove over low heat.

In a large pot over high heat, boil the fresh pasta in salted water for 3 to 4 minutes. (If you're using dry pasta, cook to al dente according to the instructions on the package.) Drain the pasta, reserving 1 cup of cooking water. Using tongs, transfer the pasta to the pot with the meat sauce. Add the cooking water and Parmesan and toss. Increase the heat to medium and simmer for 2 to 3 minutes until the pasta and meat sauce are fully incorporated. Serve on plates or in bowls topped with more Parmesan and the parsley or basil, if using.

BBQ Shrimp

Serves 4

2 pounds raw jumbo shrimp (heads on, shell intact if possible)

3 tablespoons Cajun seasoning, divided

2 tablespoons canola oil

½ yellow onion, chopped

2 cloves garlic, minced

¼ cup dry sherry

2 teaspoons dried rosemary

1 bay leaf

3 cups chicken or seafood stock

3 tablespoons Worcestershire sauce

3 tablespoons freshly squeezed lemon juice

2 teaspoons smoked paprika

8 tablespoons (1 stick) unsalted butter

1 small bunch of fresh parsley leaves, chopped

4 to 6 thick slices of French bread, grilled

In a medium bowl, toss the shrimp with 1 tablespoon of the Cajun seasoning. Cover and refrigerate for 30 minutes.

While the shrimp chills, heat the oil in a very large cast-iron skillet over medium heat. Add the onion and garlic. Cook for 5 minutes, until the onion and garlic are tender. Add the sherry and cook until the liquid evaporates, 1 minute. Add the rosemary, bay leaf, stock, Worcestershire sauce, lemon juice, paprika, and the remaining 2 tablespoons of Cajun seasoning. Bring to a boil, reduce the heat to low, and simmer until the sauce reduces by half, about 15 to 20 minutes. Pour the sauce through a wire mesh strainer over a liquid measuring cup. Reserve the strained liquid and discard the solids.

Melt the butter in the skillet. Add the shrimp and cook until they begin to turn pink, about 3 to 4 minutes. Add the reserved sauce and cook 2 to 3 more minutes, until the shrimp are done. Sprinkle with the parsley and serve with the grilled bread.

Flame-Broiled Oysters

Makes 3 dozen

1 cup (2 sticks) unsalted butter

6 cloves garlic, minced

Juice of 2 lemons

Kosher salt

Freshly ground black pepper

1 cup fresh parsley leaves, coarsely chopped

¾ cup freshly grated aged Parmesan cheese

¾ cup freshly grated aged Romano cheese

3 dozen large oysters on the half shell

1 loaf French bread, cut in half lengthwise

Preheat a grill to high heat. In a medium saucepan over medium heat, combine the butter, garlic, lemon juice, and a few pinches of salt and pepper. Cook until the butter melts. In a medium bowl, stir together the parsley, Parmesan, and Romano.

Arrange the oysters in their shells on the grill grate. Spoon the butter mixture over the oysters. Add the bread to the grill, cut sides down, and cook 30 seconds to 1 minute, until grill marks appear. Remove the bread from the grill. Cover the grill and cook the oysters 3 to 4 minutes more, until they begin to reduce in size.

Spoon the parsley mixture over each oyster, cover the grill, and cook 30 seconds to 1 minute longer, until the cheese is melted and the oysters are cooked to desired doneness. Transfer the oysters to a serving platter. Serve immediately with the bread.

Easy Chicken Thigh Skillet Dinner

Serves 6

For the chicken

6 bone-in chicken thighs, with skin

5 teaspoons Miss Brown's House Seasoning, divided (page 33)

12 ounces petite red potatoes, sliced in half

12 ounces rainbow baby carrots

2 tablespoons olive oil, plus more if needed

½ onion, sliced

2 sprigs thyme

2 sprigs fresh sage

2 sprigs fresh rosemary

1 sprig tarragon

For the butter sauce

6 tablespoons (¾ stick) unsalted butter

2 tablespoons dry sherry (optional)

1 tablespoon freshly squeezed lemon juice

2 tablespoons minced fresh parsley leaves

3 cloves garlic, minced

Kosher salt

Freshly ground black pepper

TO MAKE THE CHICKEN:
Preheat the oven to 400°F.

Season the chicken with 3 teaspoons of the House Seasoning. Season the potatoes and carrots with the remaining House Seasoning. Set aside.

In a large, heavy, oven-safe skillet or cast-iron pan over medium-high heat, warm the oil. In two batches, add the chicken, skin-side down, to the skillet and cook until brown, 4 to 5 minutes, then flip and cook the other side for 4 to 5 more minutes. Transfer the chicken to a plate.

Add the onion, potatoes, and carrots to the skillet and stir. Brown for about 4 to 5 minutes. Arrange the thyme, sage, rosemary, and tarragon evenly over the veggies. Place the chicken back in the skillet on top of the vegetables and herbs. Place in the oven on the bottom rack and bake for 40 minutes, or until the chicken and vegetables are cooked through. Remove from the oven.

TO MAKE THE BUTTER SAUCE:
Melt the butter in a small saucepan over medium heat. Add the sherry, if using, and the lemon juice, parsley, and garlic. Sprinkle with salt and pepper. Stir and bring to a slight boil. Reduce the heat to low and cook for 1 to 2 minutes, stirring. Pour over the chicken and vegetables and serve.

NOTE: *If you don't have access to fresh herbs, coat the chicken and potatoes with 2 teaspoons Italian seasoning instead.*

Slow-Cooked Brisket Sloppy Joes with Frizzled Onions

Serves 4

For the brisket

2 tablespoons olive oil

1 2-pound beef brisket, fat cap trimmed and sinew removed

1 tablespoon Miss Brown's House Seasoning (page 33)

1 medium onion, diced

1 green bell pepper, diced

2 cups beef broth

1 bay leaf

Kosher salt

Freshly ground black pepper

4 hamburger buns or bread, for serving

Pickles, for serving

For the sloppy joe sauce

1 14.5-ounce can diced tomatoes (do not drain)

2 cups ketchup

⅓ cup molasses

⅓ cup brown sugar

⅓ cup apple cider vinegar

1 tablespoon Dijon mustard

2 teaspoons sweet paprika

2 teaspoons garlic powder

½ teaspoon cayenne pepper

Kosher salt to taste

Freshly ground black pepper to taste

For the frizzled onions

½ medium red onion, sliced into 1/4-inch rings

½ cup buttermilk

1 cup all-purpose flour

Canola or vegetable oil for frying

1 teaspoon Miss Brown's House Seasoning (page 33)

TO MAKE THE BRISKET:

Preheat the oven to 300°F.

Put the olive oil in a large Dutch oven over medium-high heat. Sprinkle the brisket with the House Seasoning. Place the brisket fat-side down in the hot oil and sear until a deep golden crust forms, 5 to 7 minutes. Flip and sear the other side until deep golden brown, another 5 minutes. Transfer to a sheet tray. Add the onion and bell pepper to the Dutch oven. Stir until coated in fat. Add the beef broth and bay leaf, and bring to a boil. Put the brisket on top of the onion and pepper, season to taste with salt and black pepper, cover, and place in the oven for 3 hours.

TO MAKE THE SLOPPY JOE SAUCE:

While the brisket is slow-cooking in the oven, combine the natural juice (rendered juices from brisket), tomatoes, ketchup, molasses, brown sugar, vinegar, mustard, paprika, garlic powder, cayenne pepper, salt, and black pepper in a large saucepan. Simmer over medium-low heat until slightly thickened and reduced by a quarter, about 30 minutes.

At the 3-hour mark, pour 2 cups of the sauce over the brisket, return it to the oven, and cook until the sauce has melted into the brisket, 30 minutes more. Use a knife to test the tenderness of the brisket. It should pierce the brisket very smoothly, with no pushback. Using 2 forks, shred the meat apart. To make it sloppy, add 1 more cup of sauce.

TO MAKE THE FRIZZLED ONIONS:
Place the onion rings in the buttermilk. Put the flour in a bowl or shallow baking dish. Scoop out a few onion rings at a time and dredge them in the flour, shaking to remove any excess. In a large skillet over medium heat, heat about 1 inch oil. Add onions to the hot oil and fry until golden brown and crispy, about 4 minutes, then transfer to a wire rack on top of a baking sheet. Sprinkle with House Seasoning while still hot. Repeat with the remaining onion rings and set aside.

Assemble sandwiches with toasted or untoasted hamburger buns and brisket. Top with the frizzled onions and pickles.

Lemon Chicken Orzo Soup

Makes 10 cups

Canola, vegetable, or other neutral oil

1 ½ pound boneless, skinless chicken thighs

Heavy pinch of garlic powder

Heavy pinch of onion powder

Kosher salt

Freshly ground black pepper

1 large onion, diced

1 stalk celery, finely diced

5 teaspoons Better Than Bouillon Roasted Chicken Base

Zest of 1 lemon

Juice of 2 lemons

1 teaspoon Italian seasoning

⅓ cup chopped fresh parsley leaves, plus more for topping

1 12-ounce bag frozen carrots and peas

1 cup orzo pasta

Heat a Dutch oven or deep pot on medium-high heat. Add enough oil to cover the bottom. Season the chicken thighs with garlic powder, onion power, and a pinch of salt and pepper. Wash your hands, then add the chicken to the pot. Sear each side just until golden brown, about 4 to 5 minutes total, remove and place on a cutting board. In the same pot, add the onion and celery. You can add a little more oil if needed. Cook just until softened, about 3 to 4 minutes. Slice the chicken thighs into thin strips. Add the chicken back to the pot, add the chicken base, and sauté for an additional 4 to 5 minutes, stirring frequently. Add 5 cups water, the lemon zest, lemon juice, Italian seasoning, and fresh parsley. Taste and add salt and pepper to your liking. Turn the heat up to high and bring to a rolling boil (this will take 6 to 7 minutes). Add the frozen carrots and peas and the orzo. Boil for 8 minutes. Reduce the heat to low and cook for 4 to 5 more minutes. Serve hot with additional parsley on top.

Grilled Pork Chops with 'Mato Relish

Serves 2

For the pork chops

¼ cup finely chopped white onion
2 cloves garlic, minced
¼ cup packed brown sugar
¼ cup Worcestershire sauce
2 tablespoons apple cider vinegar
2 tablespoons vegetable oil
2 tablespoons soy sauce

1 teaspoon freshly ground black pepper
Pinch of kosher salt
2 large 1-inch-thick, bone-in pork chops (about 2 pounds total)
Handful of chopped fresh parsley leaves, for garnish

For the relish

1 cup finely diced tomato
½ yellow onion, finely diced
½ red bell pepper, finely diced
2 tablespoons sugar

2 tablespoons apple cider vinegar
1 tablespoon whole-grain mustard
Kosher salt
Pepper to taste

TO MAKE THE PORK CHOPS:

In a medium bowl, whisk together the onion, garlic, brown sugar, Worcestershire sauce, vinegar, oil, soy sauce, pepper, and salt.

Put the pork chops in a baking dish or resealable gallon-size plastic bag. Pour the marinade over the meat. Marinate for at least 1 hour at room temperature and up to 8 hours refrigerated.

Preheat an indoor grill pan to medium heat.

Grill the pork chops for 4 to 5 minutes per side, until an instant-read thermometer inserted into the thickest part of the chop registers 145°F. Let the meat rest for 5 minutes before serving. Garnish with the tomato relish and chopped parsley.

TO MAKE THE RELISH:

In a medium bowl, combine the tomato, onion, bell pepper, sugar, vinegar, and mustard. Season with salt and pepper to taste. Set aside or refrigerate until ready to serve.

Lowcountry Spaghetti

16 ounces dried or fresh spaghetti

1 tablespoon canola, vegetable, or other neutral oil

1 pound smoked sausage, such as kielbasa

8 tablespoons (1 stick) unsalted butter

6 cloves garlic, minced

1 pound lump crabmeat

1 ½ teaspoons Miss Brown's House Seasoning (page 33)

2 large beefsteak tomatoes, diced

1 cup seafood stock

½ cup dry white wine

2 tablespoons freshly squeezed lemon juice

Kosher salt, if needed

Freshly ground black pepper, if needed

1 tablespoon chopped fresh parsley leaves

Cook the spaghetti in salted water according to the package instructions, drain, and set aside.

In a large skillet over medium-high heat, add the oil and then the sausage. Sauté until browned, then add the butter to the skillet. When it melts, add the garlic and sauté for 2 to 3 minutes. Season the crabmeat with the House Seasoning. Add the crabmeat and tomatoes to the skillet and cook for an additional 2 to 3 minutes. Don't stir too much; you want to keep the lump meat intact. Pour in the seafood stock, wine, and lemon juice. Bring to a boil. Reduce the heat to medium-low and cook about 5 minutes, then taste and add salt and pepper if necessary.

Add the spaghetti to the skillet, and toss with tongs until evenly coated. Transfer the pasta and butter sauce into a large serving bowl, then top with the parsley.

Momma's Cheesy Stuffed Meatloaf

For this recipe, you'll need a 10-inch metal loaf pan. If you don't have a 10-inch pan,
you can use a 9 × 5-inch pan, but only use 1 ½ pounds of ground beef. It is crucial to let the meatloaf
rest after taking it out of the oven. If you try to slice it while it's hot, the cheese will ooze out.

Serves 6

For the meatloaf

Nonstick cooking spray

2 pounds 80/20 ground beef

1 small onion, minced

1 large egg

½ cup plain breadcrumbs

½ cup ketchup

1 tablespoon Worcestershire sauce

2 teaspoons garlic powder

Kosher salt

Freshly ground black pepper

8 ounces extra sharp yellow cheddar cheese

For the sauce

½ cup ketchup

1 teaspoon Worcestershire sauce

1 teaspoon garlic powder

2 tablespoons tomato paste

1 teaspoon Italian seasoning

Heavy pinch of sugar

Preheat the oven to 350°F. Spray a 10-inch loaf pan with nonstick cooking spray and set aside.

TO MAKE THE MEATLOAF:
In a large bowl, combine the beef, onion, egg, breadcrumbs, ketchup, Worcestershire sauce, garlic powder, a pinch of salt, and a pinch of pepper. Mix with hands until well combined. Pack half of the meat mixture tightly into the bottom of the prepared loaf pan. Add the block of cheddar cheese and then the remaining meat mixture, packing it securely. Place the pan on a rack in the middle of the oven. Place a cookie sheet on the bottom rack to catch anything that bubbles over. Bake for 45 minutes.

TO MAKE THE SAUCE:
While baking, prepare the meatloaf sauce. In a small bowl, mix the ketchup, Worcestershire sauce, garlic powder, tomato paste, Italian seasoning, sugar, and salt and pepper to taste. Increase the oven temperature to 400°F. Brush the sauce on top of the meatloaf. Return it to the oven and bake 10 minutes longer.

Remove the meatloaf from the oven and cool 15 minutes. Drain off the grease, slice the meatloaf, and serve.

Edisto Shrimp Tacos

For the shrimp tacos

1 cup buttermilk

2 tablespoons seafood seasoning, such as Old Bay, divided

½ teaspoon kosher salt

½ teaspoon freshly ground black pepper

1 ½ pounds large shrimp, cleaned and deveined

1 cup fine yellow cornmeal

1 cup all-purpose flour

Canola oil, for frying

Eight 6-inch yellow corn or flour tortillas

Lemon wedges, for serving

For southern slaw

¼ cup mayonnaise

¼ cup sour cream

2 tablespoons freshly squeezed lemon juice

3 dashes hot sauce

½ teaspoon sweet paprika

¼ teaspoon kosher salt

¼ teaspoon freshly ground black pepper

2 cups shredded red cabbage

2 cups shredded green cabbage

2 tablespoons chopped fresh parsley leaves (optional)

½ cup shredded carrot

2 scallions, sliced

TO MAKE THE SHRIMP TACOS:

Whisk together the buttermilk, 1 tablespoon of the seafood seasoning, and the salt and pepper in a medium bowl. Add the shrimp, cover, and let soak, refrigerated, for 10 to 15 minutes. While the shrimp is soaking, make the fiesta slaw.

After the shrimp has soaked, whisk together the cornmeal, flour, and remaining 1 tablespoon of seafood seasoning in a shallow dish or clean paper lunch bag. Drain the shrimp, shaking off any remaining marinade (discard the remaining marinade). Working in batches, place a few shrimp in the cornmeal mixture and flip or shake until they are coated. Transfer the shrimp to a clean plate or baking sheet. Repeat until all the shrimp have been coated.

In a large cast-iron skillet over medium-high heat, pour 1 inch of canola oil. Heat to about 375°F. Add the shrimp to the skillet a few at a time. Fry on each side until golden brown all over, 2 to 3 minutes. Remove to a cooling rack set on top of a baking sheet. Repeat with the remaining shrimp.

Toast the tortillas in a cast-iron skillet or over an open flame. Add a few shrimp to each tortilla and top with the Southern slaw. Serve with the lemon wedges.

TO MAKE THE SOUTHERN SLAW:

In a large bowl, whisk together the mayonnaise, sour cream, lemon juice, hot sauce, paprika, salt, and pepper. Add the red and green cabbage, parsley, carrot, and scallions and toss to coat.

Miss Brown's Beans and Rice

In place of the sausage, you can use hot dogs or ground beef—or no meat at all.
I'd suggest a sweet and tangy-flavored BBQ sauce for this recipe, preferably one with molasses.

Serves 6 to 8

1 tablespoon canola, vegetable, or other neutral oil

1 small onion, diced

1 green bell pepper, diced

½ pound smoked sausage, sliced ½-inch thick

2 teaspoons garlic powder

2 teaspoons sweet paprika

Kosher salt

Freshly ground black pepper

3 15.5-ounce cans pinto beans, drained but not rinsed

2 cups BBQ sauce

2 tablespoons water

1 tablespoon yellow mustard

Steamed white rice, for serving

Preheat the oven to 300°F.

Pour the oil into a large Dutch oven over medium high. Add the onion and bell pepper and sauté until the onion becomes slightly translucent, about 4 to 5 minutes. Add the meat, garlic powder, and paprika, and season with a few pinches of salt and pepper. Cook the sausage until it starts to brown, about 3 to 4 minutes. Add the beans, BBQ sauce, water, and mustard, stir, and taste. Add salt and pepper to your liking. If you like your beans soupier, add a little more water.

Cover and put the pot in the oven. Bake low and slow for 2 hours, stirring occasionally. Serve with white rice.

Red Wine–Braised Oxtails

This dish is excellent served with Creamy Sweet Potato Grits (page 220).

Serves 4 to 6

---

6 pounds oxtails (about 12 large tails)

¼ cup all-purpose flour, plus a pinch

Kosher salt

Freshly ground black pepper

2 tablespoons canola oil

3 large carrots, cut into chunks

2 stalks celery, cut into chunks

1 large white onion, cut into chunks

1 6-ounce can tomato paste

2 teaspoons Italian seasoning

1 750-milliliter bottle red wine (see Note)

3 tablespoons sugar

2 cups low-sodium beef broth

3 cloves garlic, minced

2 bay leaves

Preheat the oven to 300°F.

Coat the oxtails generously with the flour and season with salt and pepper. Heat a large Dutch oven or heavy-bottomed pot over high heat and pour in the oil. Add the oxtails in batches and brown on all sides, about 3 minutes per side. Transfer the oxtails to a plate.

While the oxtails are cooking, pulse the carrots, celery, and onion in a food processor until the vegetables are almost a puree, about 30 seconds.

Reduce the heat under the pot to medium-high, add the vegetable puree, and sauté, stirring often, until the veggies are softened, about 5 minutes. Add the tomato paste, Italian seasoning, and a pinch of flour. Cook, stirring constantly, until the tomato paste darkens slightly, about 3 minutes. Slowly pour in the wine while whisking; continue to whisk until smooth and combined. Add the sugar and bring to a boil. Reduce to a simmer and cook until the wine mixture is reduced by half, 10 to 15 minutes.

Stir in the broth, garlic, and bay leaves and bring to a boil over high heat. Turn off the stove and return the oxtails to the pot. Cover, transfer to the oven, and cook until the oxtails are tender, about 3 hours. Remove the bay leaves and serve.

NOTE: *For this recipe, use a good-quality wine that you would drink. If you would like to make this dish without alcohol, use a total of 5 cups of low-sodium beef broth instead.*

Curry Chicken Potpie

Makes 4 potpies	

1 tablespoon vegetable oil

8 tablespoons (1 stick) unsalted butter, divided

1 stalk celery, diced

½ large yellow onion, diced

1 teaspoon curry powder, preferably Madras curry powder

Kosher salt

1 clove garlic, minced

1 cup frozen peas and carrots, thawed

¼ cup all-purpose flour, plus more for the pie crust

1 ½ cups chicken broth

½ cup whole milk

Freshly ground black pepper

2 ½ cups diced cooked chicken

1 refrigerated pie crust

1 large egg, lightly beaten with 1 tablespoon water

Preheat the oven to 400°F.

Heat the oil and 6 tablespoons of the butter in a large sauté pan over medium-high heat. Add the celery, onion, curry powder, and a large pinch of salt and cook until the vegetables are soft and the onion turns translucent, about 10 minutes. Add the garlic and sauté for 1 minute, then stir in the peas and carrots. Add the flour and cook, stirring constantly, about 2 minutes. Slowly add the chicken broth and milk, whisking to remove any flour lumps. Bring to a simmer and cook until thickened, about 5 minutes. Season with salt and pepper. Add the chicken and stir to combine.

Pour the curry chicken into four 10-ounce ramekins or gratin-style bowls.

Lightly dust a clean work surface with flour. Roll out the pie crust and cut 4 circles large enough to fit over the ramekins. Lightly brush the edges of the ramekins with the egg wash. Place the pie crust circles over the top of the curry chicken, pressing to seal along the edges. Brush the top of the crust with the remaining egg wash. Using a sharp paring knife, create a few slits in the top of each potpie crust.

Bake until the crust is a deep golden brown and the potpies are bubbly, about 30 minutes. Let cool slightly before serving. Top with pats of the remaining 2 tablespoons of butter right before serving.

Creamy Sweet Potato Grits

Serves 3 to 4

2 large sweet potatoes, peeled and cut into 1-inch cubes

1 tablespoon kosher salt, plus more for seasoning

2 cups heavy cream

¾ cup yellow grits

2 teaspoons garlic powder

¼ cup grated Parmesan cheese

Freshly ground black pepper

Put the sweet potatoes in a large pot, cover with water, and add the salt. Bring to a boil over medium-high heat and cook until the potatoes are easily pierced with a knife, 10 to 15 minutes. Drain and puree the potatoes in a food processor until smooth.

Bring the heavy cream and 2 cups water to a simmer in a saucepan over medium heat. Slowly whisk in the yellow grits and garlic powder. Reduce the heat to low and continue to cook, stirring occasionally, until the grits are smooth and cooked through, about 15 minutes. Stir in the sweet potato puree and Parmesan until well combined. Season with salt and pepper.

Carolina Jambalaya

Serves 10 to 12

½ cup plus 2 tablespoons vegetable oil, divided

1 large onion, diced

1 bell pepper, diced

1 stalk celery, finely diced

Kosher salt

1 teaspoon cayenne pepper

1 pound smoked sausage, cut on a bias (I prefer Roger Wood Sausage)

1 ½ pounds dark chicken meat, cut into 1-inch cubes

2 teaspoons Miss Brown's House Seasoning (page 33)

3 cups medium-grain white rice

2 cups chicken stock

2 bay leaves

1 cup chopped scallion

Heat ½ cup of the oil in a large Dutch oven over medium heat. Add the onion, bell pepper, celery, a pinch of salt, and the cayenne pepper. Stirring often, brown the vegetables for about 20 minutes, or until they are soft and slightly caramelized. Add the sausage and cook, stirring often, for 10 to 15 minutes; with a wooden spoon, scrape the pot to loosen any browned particles.

Season the chicken with the House Seasoning. Add the chicken to the pot. Brown the chicken for 8 to 10 minutes. Add the remaining 2 tablespoons of oil, then add the rice and stir for 2 to 3 minutes to coat evenly. Slowly stir in the chicken stock plus 4 cups water and the bay leaves and cover. Cook over medium heat for 30 to 35 minutes, without stirring, or until the rice is tender and the liquid has been absorbed. Remove the pot from the heat and let stand, covered, for 5 minutes. Discard the bay leaves, top with the scallion, and serve.

Blood Orange–Glazed Salmon

¾ cup blood orange juice (from about 3 large oranges)

¼ cup agave nectar or honey

2 tablespoons canola oil

1 tablespoon sesame or olive oil

2 teaspoons soy sauce

1 teaspoon fish sauce

1 teaspoon rice wine vinegar

2 cloves garlic, minced

1 teaspoon ginger powder

4 6-ounce skin-on salmon fillets

Nonstick cooking spray

Pinch of kosher salt

Pinch of freshly ground black pepper

1 blood orange, sliced, for garnish

Preheat the oven to 450°F.

In a saucepan over medium-high heat, combine the orange juice, agave nectar, canola oil, sesame oil, soy sauce, fish sauce, vinegar, garlic, and ginger powder. Bring to a slight boil, whisking or stirring constantly. Cook for 4 to 5 minutes. Set aside.

Line a baking sheet with foil and spray with nonstick cooking spray. Brush the salmon with half of the glaze and sprinkle with the salt and pepper. Bake for 6 minutes. Add more glaze and broil for an additional 2 to 3 minutes, or until the salmon is cooked through.

Allow the salmon to rest for 2 to 3 minutes. Garnish with the orange slices. Drizzle with more sauce before serving.

Not My Momma's Cornish Hens

4 Cornish game hens, trussed

8 tablespoons (1 stick) unsalted butter, softened

⅔ cup maple syrup, divided

¼ cup brown sugar, divided

2 tablespoons kosher salt, plus more for sprinkling

1 teaspoon cayenne pepper

1 teaspoon garlic powder

1 teaspoon onion powder

1 teaspoon sweet paprika, plus more for sprinkling

1 teaspoon freshly ground white pepper

1 teaspoon pumpkin pie spice

½ cup dry sherry

1 cup chicken stock, divided

2 tablespoons cornstarch

Preheat the oven to 375°F. Place a wire rack on a rimmed baking sheet.

Pat the game hens dry and place on the prepared rack. In a medium bowl, mix together the butter, ⅓ cup of the maple syrup, 2 tablespoons of the brown sugar, the salt, cayenne pepper, garlic powder, onion powder, paprika, white pepper, and pumpkin pie spice. Rub the birds with the butter mixture, making sure it gets in all the cavities and under the skin. Reserve any unused butter for later. Sprinkle the hens with a little extra salt and paprika.

Roast for 30 minutes, then baste the hens with the juices at the bottom of the baking sheet or spread a little of the remaining butter mixture on them. Return to the oven and roast for another 15 to 30 minutes, or until the juices run clear and an instant-read thermometer inserted in the thigh (not touching the bone) registers 165°F. Remove the hens to a cutting board or serving tray to rest and remove the rack. Pour the dry sherry into the hot baking sheet and use a wooden spoon to scrape up any browned bits; add a little of the stock if necessary. Transfer the sherry mixture to a small saucepan over medium heat and add any remaining butter mixture. While the butter melts, whisk the cornstarch with 2 tablespoons of the chicken stock in a small bowl to make a slurry. Add the slurry and the remaining stock to the saucepan along with the remaining ⅓ cup of syrup and 2 tablespoons of brown sugar. Cook, whisking constantly, until the mixture thickens, about 5 minutes. Serve the game hens with the sweet and spicy gravy.

Sides, Salads, and More

Anyone who has ever gotten invited to a Southern cookout knows that sides and such are just as important as the barbecue. I mean, yes, technically potato salad, dirty rice, and fried green tomatoes are in supporting roles. But let's keep it one hundred: these dishes are a Big Deal like Holyfield. And they've gotta come correct.

I know in my own family, the party just doesn't get started until Aunt TC (for "Too Cute") arrives with her potato salad. It is very necessary. If you've watched my show for any length of time, you know how I feel: sides, salads, and sandwiches cannot hide; they must be able to stand alone. Cousins, I know I'm not by myself. We all have that uncle who shows up just for the mac and cheese.

Don't worry. I've got you covered. These recipes take out the guesswork—I'm here to demystify the classics, like She Crab Soup (page 240) and Soul Rolls (page 229), and introduce some creative newbies like Miss Brown's Famous Lasagna Dip (page 252), which you're gonna love, trust me. These are the dishes you can bring to the potluck with pride.

Soul Rolls

For the rolls

2 tablespoons extra-virgin olive oil

2 cups collard greens, cut into ¼-inch ribbons

2 cups shredded green cabbage

½ cup shredded carrot

½ medium onion, thinly sliced

½ teaspoon kosher salt

½ teaspoon freshly ground black pepper

2 cloves garlic, minced

3 tablespoons low-sodium soy sauce

1 teaspoon sesame oil

1 teaspoon rice wine vinegar

¼ teaspoon liquid smoke

2 tablespoons thinly sliced scallions

½ cup canned black-eyed peas, rinsed and drained

Canola oil, for frying

8 egg roll wrappers

For the pepper jelly sauce

½ cup pepper jelly, see Hot Peppa Jelly (page 164) or use store-bought

2 teaspoons hot sauce

2 teaspoons low-sodium soy sauce

1 teaspoon sesame oil

1 teaspoon rice wine vinegar

TO MAKE THE ROLLS:

Heat the olive oil over medium heat in a wok or large skillet. Add the collard greens, cabbage, carrot, onion, salt, and pepper and sauté until wilted and beginning to soften, 4 to 5 minutes. Add the garlic and cook another minute. Turn up the heat to medium-high and add the soy sauce, sesame oil, vinegar, and liquid smoke and cook until the liquid is absorbed, 1 to 2 minutes. Turn off the heat, then add the scallions and black-eyed peas. Transfer to a bowl and let cool completely.

In a deep skillet or enameled cast-iron pot, heat 2 inches of canola oil to 350°F. Place a wire rack on top of a sheet tray.

Lay an egg roll wrapper on a cutting board, oriented in a diamond shape. Add about an eighth of the vegetable mixture (a generous ⅓ cup) horizontally across the wrapper, in a line going from one corner to another. With your finger, moisten the edges of the wrapper with a little water. Fold the bottom corner up over the filling, then fold in the ends and roll up the wrapper, making sure it is sealed. Set aside and repeat with the remaining wrappers and filling.

Fry the rolls in batches, flipping once, until golden brown, 2 to 3 minutes. Transfer to the wire rack to drain. Serve warm with pepper jelly sauce.

TO MAKE THE PEPPER JELLY SAUCE:

In a small bowl, whisk together the pepper jelly, hot sauce, soy sauce, sesame oil, and vinegar and set aside. Serve in small bowls for dipping.

Aunt Ann's Chicken Salad

Makes 6 sandwiches

1 store-bought rotisserie chicken (about 3 pounds), white and dark meat finely chopped or processed in a food processor

1 stalk celery, minced

1 small yellow onion, minced

½ green bell pepper, minced

1⅓ cups mayonnaise

2 teaspoons garlic powder

1 teaspoon onion powder

¼ teaspoon celery seeds

Kosher salt

Freshly ground black pepper

6 croissants or 12 slices of bread

Iceberg or butter lettuce leaves, for serving (optional)

1 beefsteak tomato, sliced, for serving (optional)

In a medium bowl, mix together the chicken, celery, onion, bell pepper, mayonnaise, garlic powder, onion powder, and celery seeds in a medium bowl; season with salt and pepper. Cover and refrigerate until chilled, about 30 minutes.

Serve on split croissants with lettuce and tomato, if using.

Cheesy Smoked Pasta Salad

Serves 10 to 12

1 ½ cups mayonnaise

½ cup Asiago cheese, grated, plus more for topping

¼ cup sour cream

1 tablespoon white vinegar

3 cloves garlic, minced

2 teaspoons smoked paprika, plus more for topping

Kosher salt

Freshly ground black pepper

1 pound penne pasta, cooked

2 cups fresh baby spinach, thinly sliced

1 16-ounce jar roasted red pepper strips, drained

1 8-ounce block smoked mozzarella cheese, cubed

2 tablespoons dried parsley, for garnish

In a large bowl, whisk the mayonnaise, Asiago, sour cream, vinegar, garlic, smoked paprika, and a heavy pinch of salt and pepper.

In another large bowl, combine the cooked pasta, spinach, and roasted red pepper. Fold in the mayonnaise mixture and smoked mozzarella. Taste and add more salt and pepper if needed. Transfer to a serving bowl and chill for at least 1 hour. Before serving, toss and top with the parsley, a little grated Asiago, and a sprinkling of smoked paprika.

Southern Mac and Cheese

Serves 8 to 10

---

4 tablespoons (½ stick) unsalted butter, plus more for greasing the dish

1 pound elbow macaroni

¼ cup all-purpose flour

2 cups whole milk

½ cup heavy cream

4 ounces cream cheese

16 ounces sharp cheddar cheese, shredded, divided

1 teaspoon garlic powder

½ teaspoon kosher salt

¼ teaspoon freshly ground black pepper

2 large eggs

½ cup sour cream

1 ½ cups cubed extra sharp cheddar cheese (½-inch cubes)

Preheat the oven to 350°F. Grease a 9 × 13-inch baking dish with butter.

Bring a large pot of salted water to a boil, add the macaroni, and cook, stirring occasionally, until al dente, about 7 minutes. Strain in a colander, run cold water over the pasta, and set aside.

Using the same pot the macaroni was cooked in, melt the butter over medium heat, add the flour, and whisk until smooth. While whisking constantly, slowly add the milk and then the cream. Bring to a simmer, add the cream cheese and all but ½ cup of the shredded cheddar, and stir until melted. Stir in the garlic powder, salt, and pepper. Remove the cheese sauce from the heat and stir in the macaroni.

Whisk together the eggs and sour cream in a small bowl and then fold the egg mixture into the macaroni and cheese. Spread into the prepared baking dish, fold in the cubed cheddar, and top with the reserved ½ cup shredded cheddar. Bake until the top just begins to brown, about 20 minutes. Loosely cover with foil and bake for 10 to 15 minutes more.

Roasted Okra with Bacon Dressing

6 slices thick-cut bacon

Juice of 1 ½ lemons

1 tablespoon maple syrup

2 teaspoons Dijon mustard

Pinch of kosher salt

Pinch of freshly ground black pepper

1 pound fresh okra, cut in half lengthwise

1 tablespoon canola oil, if needed

1 teaspoon Miss Brown's House Seasoning (page 33)

Preheat the oven to 450°F.

Cook the bacon in a large cast-iron or nonstick, oven-safe skillet over medium heat until crisp, about 8 minutes. Transfer the bacon to paper towels to drain, reserving the drippings in a mixing bowl. Add the lemon juice, maple syrup, Dijon mustard, salt, and pepper to the bacon drippings. Whisk to combine. Set aside.

Crumble the bacon when cool. Set aside.

Put the okra in the skillet and add the oil if the skillet is dry. Sprinkle with the House Seasoning and toss to coat. Place the skillet on the middle rack of the oven and roast until crispy and golden brown, about 15 to 20 minutes. Remove from the oven, transfer to a serving platter, drizzle with the dressing, and top with the crumbled bacon. Serve warm.

Grandma's Green Beans

1 pound smoked turkey tails or wings and turkey leg

1 yellow onion, diced

1 tablespoon kosher salt

2 teaspoons freshly ground black pepper, divided

3 to 4 large red or Yukon gold potatoes, peeled and diced into 1-inch pieces

2 pounds fresh green beans, trimmed

4 tablespoons (1/2 stick) unsalted butter

2 cloves garlic, minced

Place the turkey tails and onion in a 4-quart Dutch oven and fill halfway with water. Season the water with the salt and 1 teaspoon of the pepper. Bring the water to a boil, then cover and simmer over low heat until the meat falls off the bones, about 2 hours. Remove and discard the bones and skin while leaving the water in the pot; return the meat to the pot.

Add the potatoes and green beans to the Dutch oven and simmer until the green beans are very tender and the potatoes can be pierced easily with a knife, about 20 minutes.

Meanwhile, melt the butter in a small skillet, then add the garlic and the remaining 1 teaspoon of pepper, and cook for 2 minutes. When the beans and potatoes are done, transfer from the pot to a serving dish with a slotted spoon and drizzle with the garlic butter.

She Crab Soup

8 tablespoons (1 stick) unsalted butter

1 medium onion, diced

1 stalk celery, diced

⅓ cup all-purpose flour

1 teaspoon seafood seasoning, such as Old Bay

¼ teaspoon grated nutmeg

1 bay leaf

Freshly ground black pepper to taste

⅓ cup dry sherry

⅓ cup clam juice

3 cups seafood stock

½ cup crab roe, plus a little more for garnish (optional)

2 cups heavy cream, at room temperature

1 teaspoon Worcestershire sauce

Kosher salt

1 pound lump blue crabmeat

In a large pot or Dutch oven, melt the butter over medium heat. Add the onion and celery and cook, stirring occasionally, until the onion is soft and translucent, about 10 minutes.

Reduce the heat to medium-low, whisk in the flour and continue to cook, stirring constantly. (You are essentially making a roux without browning it.) Stir in the seafood seasoning, nutmeg, bay leaf, and pepper, then whisk in the sherry and clam juice. Increase the heat to medium and bring to a simmer. Cook, stirring frequently, until very thick, about 10 minutes. Stir in the seafood stock and crab roe, if using. Bring to a simmer and cook for 15 minutes.

Add the heavy cream and Worcestershire sauce, return to a simmer, and cook until thickened and reduced slightly, another 15 minutes. Remove the bay leaf, then puree the soup with an immersion blender until smooth. (If using a regular blender, let the soup cool slightly first, and use caution when blending hot liquids.) Season with salt. Stir in the crabmeat and garnish with crab roe, if using.

Dirty Rice

Serves 6

3 tablespoons canola oil, divided
2 cups long-grain and wild rice mix, rinsed
3 cups chicken stock
Kosher salt
1 tablespoon unsalted butter
1 large sweet onion, finely diced
1 green bell pepper, finely diced
1 stalk celery, finely diced

2 cloves garlic, minced
16 ounces country pork breakfast sausage, such as Jimmy Dean
1 teaspoon dried thyme
1 teaspoon rubbed sage
Freshly ground black pepper
2 tablespoons minced fresh chives

Heat 2 tablespoons of the oil in a large saucepot over medium-high heat. Add the rice and cook, toasting until the rice begins to smell nutty, about 5 minutes. Add the chicken stock and a pinch more salt and bring to a boil, then reduce heat to a simmer and cover. Simmer until the rice is tender and has absorbed all the liquid, about 25 minutes. Turn off the heat.

Meanwhile, heat the remaining 1 tablespoon of oil and the butter in a large skillet over medium-high heat. Add the onion, pepper, celery, and a generous pinch of salt and cook until just tender and beginning to brown, about 5 minutes. Add the garlic, sausage, thyme, and sage and cook, breaking the sausage up with a wooden spoon until browned and cooked through, 4 to 5 minutes more.

Add the sausage and vegetables to the pot of rice. Season with a pinch of pepper. Stir gently with a fork to fluff the rice and combine. Transfer to a serving dish and sprinkle with the chives before serving hot.

Succotash

1 15-ounce bag frozen baby lima beans, thawed, or about 2 cups fresh lima beans

4 slices bacon, divided

2 tablespoons unsalted butter

1 Vidalia or sweet onion, diced

2 cups fresh corn kernels (from about 3 ears)

3 cloves garlic, minced

½ teaspoon kosher salt

½ teaspoon freshly ground black pepper

1 ½ cups frozen sliced okra, thawed

1 cup grape tomatoes

Juice of 1 lemon

2 tablespoons fresh parsley leaves, chopped, for garnish

Place the lima beans and 1 slice of bacon in a medium saucepan; cover with water. Bring to a boil over medium-high heat, then turn the heat to medium-low and simmer until the beans are just tender, 8 to 10 minutes. Drain the beans and set aside. Discard the strip of bacon with the water (it is only used for flavoring).

Meanwhile, add the remaining 3 slices of bacon to a large cast-iron skillet over medium-high heat. Cook, turning occasionally, until crispy, about 8 minutes. Transfer the bacon to a paper towel–lined plate or bowl and set aside, reserving the bacon fat in the skillet. Crumble the bacon when cool.

Melt the butter in the skillet with the bacon fat. Add the onion and cook until softened, 2 to 3 minutes. Add the corn and garlic and season with the salt and pepper. Cook until the corn is just barely done, 3 to 4 minutes. Stir in the okra and cook until tender, 2 to 3 more minutes. Add the tomatoes and drained beans and continue to cook until the corn is tender, 2 to 3 minutes. Add the lemon juice, then taste for seasoning. Top with the crumbled bacon and parsley before serving.

Roasted Garlic and Sour Cream Mashed Potatoes

Serves 6

1 head garlic

1 teaspoon olive oil

Kosher salt

2 pounds russet potatoes, washed, quartered, and peeled

6 tablespoons (¾ stick) salted or unsalted butter

½ cup sour cream

¼ cup heavy cream

Freshly ground black pepper

Preheat the oven to 400°F. Peel the papery outer layer of the garlic, then cut about ¼ inch off the top of the head. Drizzle the olive oil over the garlic and sprinkle with salt. Loosely wrap in foil and roast for 30 to 40 minutes, or until the garlic is very soft and golden. Remove from the oven and set aside.

Put the potatoes in a large pot over high heat, cover with water, add a liberal amount of salt, and bring to a boil. Lower the heat to medium-low and simmer for 15 minutes, or until fork-tender.

Drain the potatoes and return them to the pot. Squeeze the roasted garlic cloves from the head into the pot. With a potato masher, mash the potatoes and garlic until there are no large chunks. Add the butter, sour cream, and heavy cream to the pot with the potatoes and garlic and season with salt and pepper. Mash until the cream and butter are incorporated and the potatoes have a creamy consistency with some lumps. Serve warm.

Fried Cabbage

Serves 6 to 8

3 slices bacon, chopped
1 tablespoon canola oil, if needed
1 medium onion, sliced
1 large carrot, julienned
1 medium red bell pepper, sliced
1 large yellow bell pepper, sliced

1 large head green cabbage (about 3 pounds), roughly chopped
1 clove garlic, minced
1 tablespoon hot sauce
Kosher salt
Freshly ground pepper to taste

Heat a very large cast-iron skillet over medium-high heat. Add the bacon and cook until browned, 5 to 6 minutes. Transfer the bacon to paper towels, reserving the drippings in the skillet.

Add the oil to the pan if needed. Add the onion, carrot, and red and yellow peppers and cook for 5 minutes, until the vegetables begin to soften. Stir in the cabbage and garlic and sauté for 10 minutes, until the cabbage begins to brown.

Stir in the hot sauce. Bring to a boil. Cover, reduce the heat to low, and simmer until the cabbage is tender, 15 minutes. Stir in the reserved bacon, and season with salt and pepper to taste.

Sheet Pan Roasted Veggies

Serves 8

Nonstick cooking spray

1 ½ pounds baby red potatoes, washed and cut lengthwise

½ pound baby carrots, cleaned, peeled, and halved lengthwise

1 red onion, sliced

1 large rutabaga, peeled and cut into 1-inch cubes

1 medium parsnip, peeled and cut into 1-inch cubes

½ pound red beets, peeled, trimmed, washed, and cut into 1-inch wedges

2 heads garlic, tops cut off

¼ cup canola, vegetable, or other neutral oil

2 to 3 sprigs rosemary leaves plus more for garnish (optional)

2 to 3 sprigs thyme leaves plus more for garnish (optional)

2 tablespoons Miss Brown's House Seasoning (page 33)

Heat the oven to 425°F. Spray a sheet pan with nonstick cooking spray.

In a large bowl, combine the potatoes, carrots, onion, rutabaga, parsnip, beets, and garlic. Toss with the oil, rosemary, thyme, and House Seasoning.

Spread the vegetables evenly on the prepared sheet pan. Roast for 30 to 45 minutes, or until tender and golden brown. Squeeze and spread the roasted garlic heads all over the vegetables. Garnish with fresh rosemary and thyme, if using.

Lowcountry Seafood Salad

¼ cup olive oil

Juice of ½ lemon

1 pound medium shrimp, peeled and deveined

Kosher salt

Freshly ground black pepper

1 cup mayonnaise

¼ cup sweet relish

2 tablespoons red wine vinegar

2 teaspoons Dijon mustard

1 pound elbow macaroni, cooked

8 ounces crab claw meat, canned or picked for shells

5 ounces solid white tuna in oil, drained

1 stalk celery, diced

1 sweet onion, diced

½ green bell pepper, diced

¼ cup finely chopped fresh parsley leaves

Paprika, for sprinkling

Preheat a grill pan or grill to medium-high heat.

Whisk together the olive oil and lemon juice in a medium bowl. Add the shrimp to the bowl, toss to coat, and sprinkle generously with salt and pepper. Place the shrimp in the hot pan and cook for about 5 minutes, flipping once halfway through, or until the shrimp are just cooked. Set aside.

In a large serving bowl, stir together the mayonnaise, relish, vinegar, and Dijon mustard. Add the cooked pasta, shrimp, crab, tuna, celery, onion, and bell pepper and toss to combine and coat with the dressing. Season to taste with salt and pepper. Refrigerate for 1 hour or up to overnight. Sprinkle with the parsley and paprika right before serving.

Miss Brown's Famous Lasagna Dip

Serves 6 to 8

For the Italian gravy

2 tablespoons olive oil
½ medium onion, finely diced
1 small green bell pepper, finely diced
2 cloves garlic, minced
Kosher salt
1 pound Italian sausage, casings removed

½ pound ground beef
2 cups leftover pasta sauce
⅓ to ½ cup water
1 6-ounce can tomato paste
Pinch of sugar
Freshly ground black pepper

For the Parmesan béchamel sauce

2 tablespoons unsalted butter
2 tablespoons all-purpose flour
1 cup milk
⅓ cup freshly grated Parmesan cheese

1 teaspoon garlic powder
1 teaspoon Italian seasoning
Kosher salt
Freshly ground black pepper

For the dip and pasta chips

1 15-ounce container whole-milk ricotta cheese
2 cups shredded Italian-blend cheese
2 tablespoons chopped fresh parsley leaves
Vegetable oil, for frying

1 16-ounce box lasagna, cooked and patted dry
1 tablespoon garlic powder
1 tablespoon kosher salt

TO MAKE THE ITALIAN GRAVY:

Heat the oil in a large cast-iron skillet over medium-high heat. Add the onion, bell pepper, garlic, and a pinch of salt and cook until softened, about 5 minutes. Add the sausage and ground beef and cook until the meat crumbles and is no longer pink, about 4 minutes. Add the pasta sauce, water, tomato paste, sugar, and salt and pepper to taste. Reduce the heat to low and simmer for 5 to 10 minutes, until the sauce begins to thicken.

TO MAKE THE PARMESAN BÉCHAMEL SAUCE:

While the gravy cooks, melt the butter in a small saucepan over medium heat. Whisk in the flour and cook until the mixture bubbles and begins to smell nutty, about 2 minutes. Gradually whisk in the milk and cook, whisking constantly, until the mixture is thickened, about 5 minutes. Whisk in the Parmesan, garlic powder, and Italian seasoning and add salt and pepper to taste.

TO MAKE THE DIP AND PASTA CHIPS:

Preheat the oven to 375°F. Spoon the béchamel on top of the meat gravy in the skillet. Add dollops of ricotta to the top and cover with the Italian-blend cheese. Sprinkle with the chopped parsley. Bake for 30 minutes, or until golden brown and bubbly.

While the dip is in the oven, make the pasta chips. Pour the oil halfway up the sides of a very large cast-iron skillet and heat to 375°F. Cut the cooked lasagna noodles into 2-inch rectangles. Fry the pasta, in batches, until golden brown, about 4 minutes. Transfer to a paper towel-lined wire rack and sprinkle with the garlic powder and salt while still hot.

Remove the dip from the oven and serve with the pasta chips.

Fried Green Tomatoes

Serves 4

For the fried green tomatoes

1 cup all-purpose flour

3 teaspoons Miss Brown's House Seasoning (page 33), divided

2 large eggs, lightly beaten

2 tablespoons buttermilk

1 cup yellow cornmeal

Canola oil, for frying

3 green tomatoes, cut into ⅓-inch-thick slices

Kosher salt

Freshly ground black pepper

For the country sauce

½ cup mayonnaise

½ cup BBQ sauce

1 tablespoon Worcestershire sauce

1 tablespoon hot sauce

1 teaspoon Miss Brown's House Seasoning (page 33)

TO MAKE THE FRIED GREEN TOMATOES:

In a shallow pie plate or baking dish, stir together the flour and 1 teaspoon of the House Seasoning. In a separate baking dish, whisk together the eggs and buttermilk. In a third baking dish, stir together the cornmeal and the remaining 2 teaspoons of House Seasoning.

In a large cast-iron skillet, pour 1 inch of the oil and heat to 375°F over medium-high heat.

Sprinkle tomatoes with salt and pepper on both sides. Dredge one tomato slice in the flour mixture, shaking to remove any excess. Dip in the egg wash, letting any excess drip off. Coat in the cornmeal mixture and then place on a plate. Repeat with the remaining tomato slices. Working in batches, fry the tomatoes until golden brown, about 3 minutes per side. Drain on a wire rack set in a sheet tray and sprinkle with salt while still hot. Serve warm with Country Sauce.

TO MAKE THE COUNTRY SAUCE:

In a small bowl, stir together the mayonnaise, BBQ sauce, Worcestershire sauce, hot sauce, and House Seasoning.

Southern Chef Salad

Serves 8 to 12

For the cornbread croutons

Vegetable shortening or nonstick cooking spray, for the pan

1 cup all-purpose flour

1 cup plain cornmeal

2 tablespoons sugar

1 tablespoon baking powder

1 teaspoon kosher salt

1 cup buttermilk

8 tablespoons (1 stick) unsalted butter, melted

2 tablespoons vegetable or canola oil

1 large egg

Nonstick cooking spray, for the baking sheet

Olive oil, for drizzling

For the salad

1 large head green-leaf lettuce, chopped

2 slices country ham, browned and chopped

3 large hard-boiled eggs, quartered

½ cup thinly sliced red onion

1 cup julienned carrot

1 cup julienned cucumber

1 pint grape tomatoes, halved lengthwise

1 cup shredded sharp cheddar cheese

3 cups cornbread croutons

⅓ cup Creamy Carolina Vinaigrette (page 258)

TO MAKE THE CORNBREAD CROUTONS (SEE NOTE):

Preheat the oven to 400°F. Lightly grease a 9-inch baking pan with shortening or nonstick cooking spray.

In a medium bowl, combine the flour, cornmeal, sugar, baking powder, and salt. In a separate bowl, whisk together the buttermilk, butter, vegetable oil, and egg. Add the buttermilk mixture to the flour mixture, stirring just until the dry ingredients are moistened. (The batter will be lumpy and thick.)

Pour the batter into the prepared pan. Bake until a toothpick inserted in the center comes out clean, 22 to 25 minutes. Let cool on a wire rack.

The next day, preheat the oven to 350°F. Spray a baking sheet with nonstick cooking spray.

Cut the cornbread into 1-inch cubes and transfer them to a large mixing bowl. Drizzle with the olive oil and gently toss. Spread the cornbread cubes onto the prepared baking sheet in one even layer. Bake until golden brown, 15 to 20 minutes, flipping the croutons halfway through.

TO MAKE THE SALAD:

Arrange the lettuce, ham, eggs, onion, carrot, cucumber, tomatoes, cheese, and cornbread croutons on a serving platter. Drizzle with the Creamy Carolina Vinaigrette over the salad.

NOTE: *Make the cornbread 24 hours in advance, and bake the croutons the day of salad preparation.*

Creamy Carolina Vinaigrette

3 tablespoons apple cider vinegar

⅓ cup canola, vegetable, or other neutral oil

1 cup buttermilk

¼ cup mayonnaise (I prefer Duke's)

2 teaspoons Dijon mustard

⅓ cup diced Vidalia onion

1 tablespoon Miss Brown's House Seasoning (page 33)

1 teaspoon honey

Kosher salt

Freshly ground black pepper

In a blender, mix the vinegar, oil, buttermilk, mayonnaise, mustard, onion, House Seasoning, and honey until smooth. Add salt and pepper to taste. Store in a mason jar in the refrigerator for up to 2 weeks.

Seafood Mac and Cheese

Kosher salt

2 tablespoons olive oil

2 cloves garlic, minced

1 medium yellow onion, finely diced

1 pound shrimp, peeled and deveined

Freshly ground black pepper

1 pound blue or lump crabmeat, picked for shells and chopped

½ cup dry sherry

2 tablespoons unsalted butter

1 tablespoon all-purpose flour

1 pint heavy cream

1 cup milk

1 tablespoon chopped fresh parsley, plus more for sprinkling

1 tablespoon chopped fresh tarragon

1 tablespoon chopped fresh thyme

2 teaspoons dry mustard

1 teaspoon smoked paprika

4 ounces Gruyère cheese, shredded (about 1 cup)

4 ounces Parmesan cheese, shredded (about 1 cup)

12 ounces extra-sharp yellow cheddar cheese, shredded (about 3 cups), divided

1 pound elbow macaroni

4 ounces cream cheese

Preheat the oven to 375°F.

Heat a large pot of salted water, allow water to come to a boil.

While water is coming to a boil, heat the 2 tablespoons of oil in a large skillet over medium-high heat. Add the garlic and onion and cook, stirring occasionally, until they start to soften, about 5 minutes.

In a bowl, season the shrimp with salt and pepper. Transfer the seasoned shrimp and crabmeat to the skillet and cook, stirring occasionally, until the seafood starts to brown, 3 to 5 minutes. Scoop the contents of the skillet into a bowl and set aside.

Deglaze the skillet with the sherry, stirring to scrape up the browned bits from the bottom, and cook until reduced, about 5 minutes. Add the butter and, when melted, add the flour. Cook, stirring, until there are no remaining clumps. Whisk in the heavy cream, milk, parsley, tarragon, thyme, mustard, and paprika, followed by the Gruyère, Parmesan, and 2 cups of the cheddar. Bring to a simmer, then lower the heat to low and simmer for 10 minutes. Season with salt and pepper.

Meanwhile, add the macaroni to the boiling water and cook according to the package instructions. Reserve 1 cup cooking water, then drain the macaroni and return it to the pot. (I like to just leave a little pasta water in the pot when I drain it.) Add the cheese sauce, cream cheese, and

(cont.)

seafood mixture and mix well. If the mac and cheese is too stiff, add some pasta water, ¼ cup at a time. Season with more salt and pepper, if needed.

Pour the mac and cheese into a 9 × 13-inch baking dish. Layer the remaining 1 cup of cheddar evenly over the top. Bake until the cheese is nice and brown, 10 to 15 minutes. (Be careful, the cheese may bubble over in the oven.) Let rest for 15 to 20 minutes before serving. Sprinkle with parsley, if using.

NOTE: *Seafood Mac and Cheese can be made ahead. Reheat it in a 200°F oven for 15 to 20 minutes before serving.*

Black-Eyed Pea Risotto

Serves 4

6 cups chicken broth

8 tablespoons (1 stick) unsalted butter

¼ cup olive oil

1 cup finely diced yellow onion

1 14.5-ounce can black-eyed peas, drained

5 cloves garlic, minced

2 cups arborio rice

½ cup dry white wine

1 ½ cups grated Parmesan cheese

1 cup frozen green peas, thawed

Kosher salt

Freshly cracked multicolor pepper

Heat the chicken broth in a medium saucepan over medium heat, then cover and keep warm on low heat.

Melt the butter in a large saucepan over medium heat and add the olive oil. Add the onion and sauté, stirring occasionally, until tender and translucent, about 5 to 6 minutes. Add the black-eyed peas and garlic and sauté, stirring occasionally, until the peas are tender, 10 to 12 minutes.

Next, add the rice and stir to incorporate with the black-eyed peas, then immediately add the white wine. Cook, stirring often, until the liquid is absorbed, about 2 minutes. Add 1 cup of the broth to the saucepan with the rice and simmer over medium-low heat, stirring often, until the liquid is absorbed, 3 to 4 minutes. Continue to cook, adding the broth by the cupful and stirring often, until the rice is tender and creamy, 28 to 32 minutes. Stir in the Parmesan and green peas. Add salt and pepper to taste. Serve warm.

Savory Skillet Corn

4 slices thick-cut bacon

2 tablespoons unsalted butter

1 Vidalia onion, finely diced

1 green bell pepper, finely diced

6 ears corn, cut from the cob (about
3 to 4 cups)

1 ripe beefsteak tomato, diced

Kosher salt

Freshly ground black pepper

Heat a large cast-iron skillet over medium heat. Add the bacon and cook until crispy, about 3 minutes per side. Transfer the bacon from the skillet to a paper towel–lined plate. Crumble when cool.

In the same skillet containing the bacon drippings, melt the butter over medium-high heat, then add the onion and bell pepper. Cook until the veggies are softened and starting to brown, 4 to 5 minutes. Stir in the corn and tomato. Sprinkle with salt and pepper then stir. Cook for another 2 to 3 minutes, until the corn is tender and the tomato is starting to release its liquid. Stir in the crumbled bacon and remove from the heat. Serve warm.

Lowcountry Deviled Eggs

Serves 24

12 large eggs

24 large shrimp, cleaned and deveined, tail intact

3 teaspoons seafood seasoning, such as Old Bay, divided

Canola, vegetable, or other neutral oil, for grilling

⅓ cup mayonnaise

2 teaspoons Dijon mustard

2 teaspoons sweet relish

1 teaspoon garlic powder

⅛ teaspoon kosher salt

⅛ teaspoon freshly ground black pepper

2 scallions, thinly sliced

Smoked paprika, for dusting

Put the eggs in a large saucepan and cover with water. Heat over high heat until the water begins to boil. Boil for 1 minute, cover with a lid, and remove from the heat. Allow to sit for 17 minutes, then drain and transfer the eggs to an ice bath.

While the eggs are cooling, toss the shrimp with 2 teaspoons of the seafood seasoning. On an indoor grill or in a large skillet, grill the shrimp with a drizzle of oil, flipping midway through, until they are fully cooked and opaque. You want an even grill or sear on both sides. Remove from the heat, transfer to a plate, and refrigerate until ready to serve.

When the eggs are cooled, peel them and slice in half lengthwise. Transfer the yolks to a medium bowl and mash with a fork until crushed. Stir in the mayonnaise, mustard, relish, garlic powder, remaining teaspoon of seafood seasoning, salt, and pepper. Mash well. Spoon or pipe the filling (using a piping bag or resealable plastic bag) into each egg white half.

Top the deviled eggs with the cooked shrimp, scallion, and a dusting of paprika.

Beverages

Full disclosure: I am not much of a drinker. I never really developed a taste for wine or alcohol. But the South Carolina hostess in me *loves* the vibe of a fresh cocktail—with or without the likka, as they say. Who doesn't enjoy the looks of a classic southern julep?

During my New Gullah Supper Club heyday, we became known for our themed drinks, some of which I made up to complement each particular event. I was certainly not trying to get folks drunk, but imbibing was an intentional part of the supper club mood. When I entertain, I like to surprise my guests. So often the drink adds a bit of whimsy to the occasion. My Key Lime Pie Milkshake (page 273), for example, has always been a huge crowd-pleaser.

You'll find recipes for Spiked Peachy Lemonade (page 278), Ma's Blueberry Mocktail (page 274), and more. But how*ever* you choose to get your sip on, what matters most is the joy it adds!

Lowcountry Mint Julep

Serve this classic cocktail in a clear glass or julep cup.

Serves 4	
20 to 24 mint leaves	Shaved ice
2 ounces lemon simple syrup	4 lemon slices, for garnish
1 cup bourbon	4 mint sprigs, for garnish
For the lemon simple syrup	
1 cup freshly squeezed lemon juice, pulp strained	1 cup sugar
	Zest of 2 lemons
1 cup water	

Put 5 or 6 mint leaves in the bottom of each glass, and add ½ ounce lemon simple syrup to each. Muddle the mint leaves with the simple syrup by using a muddler or a wooden spoon to macerate the leaves. Doing this helps release the flavor of the mint and infuses the syrup. Add ¼ cup bourbon to each glass and mix with a cocktail stirrer. Top off with shaved ice. Garnish each cocktail with a lemon slice and a sprig of mint.

TO MAKE THE LEMON SIMPLE SYRUP:
Put the lemon juice, water, sugar, and lemon zest into a medium saucepan over medium-high heat. Bring to a boil, then lower the heat to medium and simmer, stirring frequently, until the mixture thickens, 8 to 10 minutes. Let cool, then transfer to a mason jar until ready to use. Keep refrigerated up to 6 months.

Spicy Watermelon Sangria

Serves 6

6 cups seedless watermelon, cubed

1 750-milliliter bottle sweet rosé, sweet blush, or dry rosé wine

½ cup white rum, such as Ten to One, The Real McCoy, or Bacardi

1 teaspoon cayenne pepper

2 11.15-ounce bottles Italian blood orange soda

Fresh mint leaves, for garnish

6 watermelon wedges, for garnish

Add the watermelon cubes to a blender and blend until smooth, about 2 minutes. Strain, then add the watermelon juice to a pitcher. Add the wine, rum, and cayenne pepper. Divide the sangria among 6 glasses, then top with the Italian soda. Garnish with the mint and watermelon wedges.

Swamp Water

Serves 2 or 3

½ cup lemonade

¾ cup iced tea

½ cup ginger beer (not ginger ale)

Lemon slices, for garnish

Mix the lemonade, iced tea, and ginger beer in a small pitcher or 32-ounce mason jar. Pour over ice into 2 or 3 glasses. Garnish with lemon slices.

Key Lime Pie Milkshake

6 large scoops of French vanilla ice cream (about 1 ½ cups)

1 cup sweetened condensed milk, divided

¼ cup half-and-half, or more if needed

⅓ cup fresh or bottled key lime juice

1 ½ teaspoons key lime zest, plus more for garnish

½ cup crushed graham crackers, for garnish

Whipped cream, for topping

4 key lime slices, for garnish

Place the ice cream, ¾ cup of the condensed milk, the half-and-half, lime juice, and lime zest into a high-powered blender. Blend until the milkshake reaches the desired thickness, adding more half-and-half as needed.

Place the graham cracker crumbs on a plate and pour the remaining ¼ cup of condensed milk into a small bowl. Dip the rim of each glass in the milk, then roll it in the graham cracker crumbs. Pour the milkshake evenly into four glasses, top with the whipped cream, and garnish with the key lime slices, lime zest, and additional graham crackers, if using.

Ma's Blueberry Mocktail

Serves 4	
1 cup frozen or fresh blueberries, thawed	1 750-milliliter bottle sparkling apple cider
½ cup water	Fresh blueberries, for garnish (optional)
½ cup honey	⅓ cup honey, for garnish (optional)
Juice of 1 lemon	⅓ cup sugar, for garnish (optional)

Place the blueberries in a small saucepan. Add the water, then stir in the honey. Heat over medium-high heat until the mixture comes to a low boil and the blueberries just start to break apart. Turn the heat down to low and simmer until the sauce is nicely thickened, 2 to 3 minutes. Remove from the heat and stir in the lemon juice. Strain through a mesh strainer. Set aside until ready to serve.

Place 1 tablespoon of the cooled blueberry syrup at the bottom of each champagne glass. Top with the sparkling apple cider.

To make the optional sugared blueberry garnish, coat fresh blueberries in the honey, then roll in the sugar. Place 3 sugared blueberries on a metal skewer or toothpick and use to garnish a mocktail. Repeat for each mocktail.

Palmetto Punch

2 ounces orange juice

46 ounces pineapple juice

32 ounces white cranberry juice

1 liter lemon-lime soda

Juice of 2 lemons

Lemon slices, orange slices, and fresh cranberries, for garnish

Ice cubes, for serving (optional)

Combine the orange juice, pineapple juice, cranberry juice, soda, and lemon juice in a large punch bowl. Top with the lemon and orange slices and cranberries. Ladle into glasses with ice, if using.

Spiked Peachy Lemonade

Serves 4 to 6	
Ice cubes	1 cup bourbon (optional)
4 cups store-bought or homemade lemonade	4 to 6 lemon slices, for garnish
	4 to 6 peach slices, for garnish
2 cups peach nectar	
For the peach nectar	
3 cups thawed frozen or sliced fresh peaches	2 teaspoons freshly squeezed lemon juice
	1 to 2 tablespoons sugar (optional)

In a pitcher filled with ice, stir together the lemonade, peach nectar, and bourbon, if using. Pour into iced tea glasses filled with ice and garnish with lemon slices and peach slices.

TO MAKE THE PEACH NECTAR:
Combine 2 cups water, the peaches, lemon juice, and sugar, if using, in a blender and blend until smooth. Strain the peach nectar through a fine-mesh strainer. Store in an airtight container in the refrigerator for up to two days. Makes 1 quart.

ACKNOWLEDGMENTS

This is my very first cookbook and it wasn't easy. I can't say I traveled this journey alone and there are some very special people who helped me along the way. I'd like to take the time to thank those folks now.

To my mom and grandma, I don't think saying thank you will suffice. I could never repay you both for what you've done and scarified for me. I've dedicated my life's work to you. I love you so very much!

The love of my life, Bryon, I thank you. When I felt I lost my spark, you gave me another reason to get back in the kitchen and cook. You are my guinea pig, taste tester, but most of all you're my best friend. I love doing this thing called life with you.

My editor, Patrik Bass. Thank you for sending that cold email in March of 2020. I'm a strong believer in fate and divine timing. You, sir, were sent to me at the perfect time! Little do you know that email changed the trajectory of my career. Because of you I can proudly say I AM a cookbook author. Thank you for taking a chance on me. I'd also like to thank Amistad/HarperCollins for publishing *The Way Home*.

My agents, Eve, Jon, Danielle, and Jeff. Thank you all so much for your professional guidance. Eve, as my literary agent you have been such an instrumental part of this entire process. Your gentle spirit really helped me feel more at ease because I was literally terrified LOL.

Ylonda Gualt, my girl! Energy means everything to me and your energy felt like home. It didn't take me long to figure out that you were the right woman for the job. Thank you so much for eloquently putting my life, thoughts, and words on paper. I now have sista for life!

Ashley Strickland Freeman, thank you so much for styling and testing my recipes. You are a powerhouse and I admire you in so many ways. I'm one lucky gal to have you on my culinary team!

My man Sully Sullivan! Not everyone gets me, but you do. From the moment I met you and I saw those quirky Biggie Smalls socks you were wearing, I just knew we would hit it off! Your eye for photography is unmatched. And you know how to bring out the best in anything you photograph. Thanks for bringing my vision to life, brother.

Miss Angela Hall, thank you for styling my cookbook shoot. You have an undeniable talent and you helped make my cookbook that much more beautiful.

Julia and John, thank you both so much for your help during the shoot. You went above and beyond to make sure the shoot went as seamlessly as possible.

My glam squad, Ange, Valisha, and Yolanda, thank you all from the bottom of my heart for making me feel and look so beautiful. We have a special bond that I do no not take for granted! I love y'all!

To my Discovery/Food Network family, thank you for giving this Geechee girl from Charleston, South Carolina a shot. I am forever grateful!

Thanks to my soul tribe. My best friends and family who've supported me throughout this entire journey of exploration. It really does take a village and I have a darn good one!

Finally, I would like to thank you all, my cousins. I call you all "cousins" for a reason. You're not just fans to me, you are very much a part of my family and story. Many of you all have watched me grow over the years. It's only right that I acknowledge you all as well. None of this would be possible without your continued support. Thank you!

With love,
Kardea

UNIVERSAL CONVERSION CHART

Oven Temperature Equivalents

$250°F = 120°C$

$275°F = 135°C$

$300°F = 150°C$

$325°F = 160°C$

$350°F = 180°C$

$375°F = 190°C$

$400°F = 200°C$

$425°F = 220°C$

$450°F = 230°C$

$475°F = 240°C$

$500°F = 260°C$

Measurement Equivalents

Measurements should always be level unless directed otherwise.

⅛ teaspoon = 0.5 mL

¼ teaspoon = 1 mL

½ teaspoon = 2.5 mL

1 teaspoon = 5 mL

1 tablespoon = 3 teaspoons = ½ fluid ounce = 15 mL

2 tablespoons = ⅛ cup = 1 fluid ounce = 30 mL

4 tablespoons = ¼ cup = 2 fluid ounces = 60 mL

5 ⅓ tablespoons = ⅓ cup = 3 fluid ounces = 80 mL

8 tablespoons = ½ cup = 4 fluid ounces = 120 mL

10 ⅔ tablespoons = ⅔ cup = 5 fluid ounces = 160 mL

12 tablespoons = ¾ cup = 6 fluid ounces = 180 mL

16 tablespoons = 1 cup = 8 fluid ounces = 240 mL

INDEX

ABOUT THE AUTHOR

KARDEA BROWN is a contemporary southern cook and the host of Food Network's *Delicious Miss Brown*, currently in its sixth season, and of *The Great Soul Food Cook-Off*, a collaboration between OWN and Discovery+. Of Gullah Geechee descent, a term used to describe a distinct group of African Americans who are preserving their West African language, culture, and cuisine, and live in the coastal areas of South Carolina and Georgia, Kardea spent a significant portion of her childhood on Wadmalaw Island, surrounded by the Gullah community. *Delicious Miss Brown* films at her family's home on Edisto Island, where she shares the rich history of her Gullah heritage and its cuisine with viewers, often featuring a signature twist. Kardea got her first break when she filmed the pilot of *Deen of Lean* alongside Bobby Deen, and thereafter created the New Gullah Supper Club pop-up, a traveling dinner series with a menu that pays homage to the dishes passed down from her grandmother and mother. She has also appeared on various Food Network shows including *Beat Bobby Flay*, *Chopped Junior*, *Cooks vs. Cons*, *Family Food Showdown*, and *Farmhouse Rules*. Kardea's first book, *The Way Home: A Celebration of Sea Islands Food and Family*, is part autobiography and part cookbook, exploring her personal history and Gullah heritage and sharing recipes for Lowcountry dishes and lighter Gullah fare.

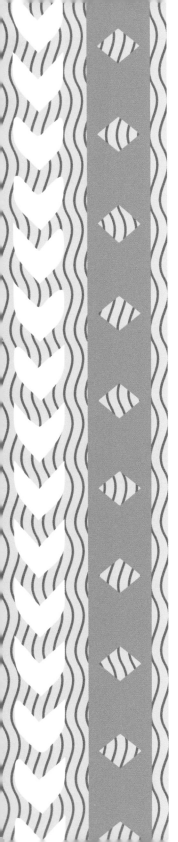

HarperCollins books may be purchased for educational, business, or sales promotional use. For information, please email the Special Markets Department at SPsales@harpercollins.com.

FIRST EDITION

Designed by Bonni Leon Berman

All photography by Sully Sullivan unless otherwise noted.

Page x (bottom right): Dan Xeller
Pages 4, 7, 10: Courtesy of the author
Page 24 (two photos on the bottom right): Dan Xeller
Page 27 (bottom left): Food Network
Page 80: Gordon Bell

Library of Congress Cataloging-in-Publication Data has been applied for.

ISBN 978-0-06-308560-2

22 23 24 25 26   LSC   10 9 8 7 6 5 4 3 2 1